Wakefield Press

Adopting
Parents' Stories

Adopting

Parents' Stories

edited by Jane Turner Goldsmith

Wakefield
Press

Part proceeds from the sale of this anthology will be directed to support
adoptive parents and their children.

Wakefield Press
1 The Parade West
Kent Town
South Australia 5067
www.wakefieldpress.com.au

First published 2007

Designed by Liz Nicholson, designBITE
Typeset by Clinton Ellicott, Wakefield Press
Printed and bound by Hyde Park Press, Adelaide

National Library of Australia
Cataloguing-in-publication entry

Adopting: parents' stories.

ISBN 978 1 86254 768 1 (pbk.).

1. Adoptive parents – Australia - Interviews. 2. Intercountry adoption –
Australia – Case studies. I. Turner Goldsmith, Jane.

362.734092294

**Government
of South Australia**

Arts SA

fox creek

To my wonderful parents, Tom and Jan,

and to all parents.

Contents

Conflict

Journey

Challenge

Preface

Jane Turner Goldsmith

Who are you, I wonder, the person browsing this book? Are you a parent, a would-be parent, or are you an adoptee? Perhaps you are looking for stories that reflect your own experience in adoption, or considering adoption after a failure to conceive naturally or through IVF. The stories in this anthology are primarily the experiences of adoptive parents, though if you are an adoptee, you may be interested to read of parents' journeys when deciding to adopt.

The idea for this collection came to me when I was asked to present a workshop in Adelaide at the 8th Australian Conference on Adoption in April 2004. As a psychologist working with an adoption agency, my job was to assess the couple's suitability to adopt a child from overseas. I had encountered many compelling stories during my interviews with prospective adoptive parents. The emotions we explored seemed to span the entire range of human experience: dreams, loss, grief, hope, conflict, challenge. Yet I was unable to lay my hands on suitable parent-friendly literature that reflected the Australian context of adoption, and from the point of view of the adopting parent. Stories by adult adoptees were available; in fact the recent volume *The Colour of Difference* (ed. Sarah Armstrong, Federation Press, 2001), which contains stories from the hearts of adult adoptees, inspired me to gather experiences from this other perspective: that of parents seeking to adopt a child.

Thinking back to that invitation to run a workshop I had to ask myself, too, what I could contribute. I had no personal experience; though a parent, I had not adopted nor been in a position to consider adoption as a means of creating a family. I felt the people I interviewed were the real experts. I could try my best to identify with some of those powerful emotions of loss and challenge that people related during our discussions.

As a writer and a teacher, though, I felt I had something to contribute. I wanted to hear and record the voices of parents themselves. Perhaps I could facilitate a process that is regarded by many as therapeutic – the 'telling of story'.

And so this anthology began. I ran a workshop at the conference at which about a dozen delegates shared their experience of becoming parents. I was grateful to those dozen people for advertising the project in their own states, through their adoption networks. Eventually I had a pool of 40 or more potential contributors, and many stories spanning the nation. From the start I had set out to record not only the joys but the challenges and difficulties that parents face, from the moment they start to consider adoption, through to the ongoing (actually never-ending) process of raising a child. I wanted parents to talk about the tough times, the grieving, the frustrations, the misgivings, the pain, the guilt, the reactions of friends and families, the ethical and moral dilemmas they faced, and their moments of doubt.

Not surprisingly, as stories started to come in, I found those whose authors were prepared to expose their vulnerabilities the most compelling of all. I started an e-mail dialogue with these writers, probing their hearts for more of the tough stuff, detail I thought they may have glossed over or avoided, more insights into the times when they had been most confronted by their own emotions or the reactions of others. Stories that had scrubbed off the warts were returned requesting those warts be reinstated! Warts are required in order to tell the real story.

The stories have been gathered under themes. There are stories of dreams, hope, journeys and joy. There are also stories of grief, loss, conflict and challenge. I acknowledge that each story encompasses many, if not all, of the above themes within the one account. As a whole, though, I hope the reader will appreciate the stages that, it seems, parents commonly move through in the process of adopting.

Not all have happy endings; some are painful to read. We

know there are risks when adopting a child who may have spent their early months or years in an orphanage or in difficult family circumstances. Unfortunately, in some of these cases, an adoption breaks down or the family finds itself under significantly greater stress than anyone anticipated. Some parents were brave enough to write about these traumas and I commend them for their honesty in sharing their difficult and sometimes unbearably sad experiences for the benefit of others. If you read these stories carefully, though, you may also hear the voice that says if given their time again, there is little they would change or trade. I hope, too, that you will find, as I did, that voice of optimism, of unshakeable faith in the strength of the human spirit.

We are lucky to have contributors who adopted a few decades ago in Australia when local adoptions were the norm, when couples had 24 hours to organise the nursery in time for their newborn's arrival. However, most of the stories reflect the current context of adoption in Australia – intercountry adoption (warts and all). The stories take us to India, Korea, the Philippines, Thailand, Romania, China, Ethiopia and Indonesia.

With the exception of Romania and Indonesia, these are the main countries with whom Australia currently maintains ongoing adoption programmes. There are approximately 500 intercountry adoptions each year, representing about three quarters of total adoptions within Australia. Each state has their own Act regulating the processes of adoption, and the programmes and protocols with overseas countries also vary. For example, if a couple adopts from Korea, it is likely that the baby to be adopted has been relinquished to foster care by a young, unwed mother in a society that disapproves of illegitimacy and provides no resources for single mothers. In China, the one-child policy and society's favouring of male offspring means that there are many more abandoned baby girls ending up in orphanages and available for adoption to Western families. In both of these countries, younger children are more likely to be available for adoption, whereas in India or Ethiopia, it is more likely that older children, or sibling groups who have lost family supports through adverse life circumstances, become available for adoption. Societal factors in any of these countries, and consequently their adoption programmes, quotas and regulations, may all change within a short space of time. It is beyond the scope of this anthology to provide specific detail on the different programmes, and any insights the reader may gain regarding 'process' should not be considered the official word. Readers interested in adopting from overseas should seek current, up-to-date information directly from the adoption services in their own state. The Attorney-General's Internet page on intercountry adoption is recommended as a good starting point, as it directs readers to the authorities in each state: (www.ag.gov.au/www/agd/agd.nsf/Page/Families_Children_ Intercountryadoption).

I hope that the stories in this anthology will raise as many questions as they answer for prospective adoptive parents, for the decision to adopt is not one that can be considered without a thorough appreciation of potential challenges and risks – moral, psychological, cultural and practical. I believe parents *do* need to question and confront: whether they are doing the right thing and how they will manage the bureaucracy, the foreign country, the Third-World orphanage, the lack of information about the child, attachment, maintaining the birth country's culture and the role of the biological family. All of these challenges, and more. Reading the stories of those who have gone before can help prospective adoptive parents to clarify in their own minds the significance of the many factors that must be considered in a life-changing choice such as adoption.

As we go to press, international adoption is fraught with controversy. There are widely differing ethical and moral viewpoints. Some believe that no child should ever be taken from their birth country and culture, no matter the abuse, poverty and vulnerability of their life circumstances. Others believe that provided all avenues for support within the birth country have been exhausted, intercountry adoption is the next-best and most-humane option. This anthology does not seek to assert any particular position, nor to add fuel to that debate; it seeks more to record accurately the voices of parents who have been through the experience.

The contributors to this anthology come from all walks of life; they represent 'ordinary' Australian people who have done 'extraordinary' things. This is the first publication for some, while others are experienced writers. It has been an added satisfaction for me to have been able to encourage new writers to tell their stories. Many of the authors, too, have expressed their satisfaction at having had the opportunity to process their experiences and to know that their voices will be heard. Some of the contributors have chosen to use pen names, either for themselves or for their children.

I would like to extend a special thank you to all of the contributors, who have been willing to share their experiences for the benefit of future adoptive parents.

Dreams

But I do want to have a child, with an innate and deeply ingrained part of my being.

Why would you want to do it?

Julia Rollings

I think it's wonderful but why would you want to do it? Do you get money from the government? I'd heard these questions before. The tone and words may change, but not the incredulity.

The boys were past the age when their countrymen were likely to adopt them so their orphanage sent details overseas to seek a family. Whether fate or God brought us all together I don't know. I hate to think it was simply chance.

Two little boys had lost their first family. Domestic stress and poverty had weakened the bonds between their parents. Their mother was banished, along with their brother and sister. The boys' misery was compounded when their father, having taken them by rail halfway across India, abandoned them at a station platform while they slept.

The children clung to each other at the local orphanage where they were taken by police. The head of the orphanage, 'mother' to 300 orphaned and abandoned children, told me how she remembered Madhu as he carried Sadan and cried constantly for the first few months. He slept with his baby brother and cared for him through the day.

One day the boys were called to the office and shown our photos. 'They are your new mother and father,' Madhu was told. He argued. He knew what his parents looked like, and we weren't even the right colour. 'You will be going on a plane,' he was told, but was offered nothing about Australia and he had no real understanding of adoption.

When Barry and I married, I already had a two-year-old daughter, Alix, and Barry was the father of four teenage children. Barry became Alix's adoptive father and we then had a baby daughter, Briony, together. Though we already had a fairly large family, we felt there was room in our lives and our hearts for more children. Barry's daughters and son were approaching adulthood and our home felt rather quiet with only two children.

We already loved each other's children, so we felt confident about our ability to love children not born to us. We also felt we'd rather look at parenting children who didn't have a family, than have more children ourselves. So when Alix was seven and Briony three, we brought home from Korea our five-month-old son Haden, a chubby little boy who was always smiling. Two years later we adopted two-year-old Joel, from Taiwan. Joel had waited for a family for some time because he was born blind. A few years later we decided we would like to adopt again, so we started looking for other children who were waiting for parents. That is when we heard about Madhu and Sadan, and felt hopeful they might like to join our family.

With guardianship granted and passports issued Alix, now 13, and I arrived in India at the beginning of the hot season. Within a few weeks the international news would talk of the numbers dying in the heatwave.

Sights and smells assailed my senses in those first few days. I knew of the poverty and expected it, but I still felt shocked. But I was also amazed by the dignity and strength of character of the people, given their circumstances. How could a family living in a slum under cardboard and black plastic still smile as we walked past? Most people were helpful and friendly, and the country fascinating. Although I was a woman travelling alone with my daughter I didn't feel threatened or in danger, despite my relative wealth.

We arrived at the orphanage in the heat of the afternoon and the boys were brought to meet us in the office. They were much smaller than I expected and obviously scared. Sadan, a five-year-old boy smaller than a two-year-old, was lifted onto my lap. He sat there stiffly, and it took a lot of effort to raise a weak smile from him. Madhu wouldn't look at us and soon burst into tears. So these were my sons; boys I had daydreamed about for more than a year since I had first seen their photo. I longed to hug them and kiss away their tears, but I had to put my feelings on hold and take things at their pace. This was a profound moment for me, but I could see they had no idea what was happening, or what they should do.

I was told I could take them but decided to visit over a couple of days to make it easier. Eventually we had to leave and I put two scared little boys into the taxi with me and returned to our hotel. The boys sat on the floor of the hotel room, the gifts I had brought for them untouched except for a packet of Smarties quickly eaten by Sadan. Practicalities had to be taken care of and the boys stood in the bathtub as we tried to wash out their lice. It took a couple of days to convince all the little critters to curl up and die.

Madhu and Sadan slept on the double bed next to me, their arms wrapped tightly around each other in sleep. I lay quietly next to them, studying their faces and taking in their unfamiliar smell. They were obviously closely attached to each other and I wondered whether the two of them would ever be able to form that kind of attachment to me and their new father. It choked me up to know that if they hadn't found a family they were due to be separated. To avoid complications with the teenage girls, boys can stay in the orphanage only until they are nine or ten years old. Madhu was allowed to stay longer because his adoption was in progress. What a tragedy it would have been if the brothers had been separated after already losing the rest of their family. As they lay peacefully sleeping, I wondered what other traumas they had already experienced and whether they would be able to accept the love of a new family.

We stayed in India another three weeks, seeing the most famous sights and meeting some lovely people. The boys spoke no English and my halted attempts at their language were usually unsuccessful. Necessity expedited things though, and in a couple of days the boys learned what they considered the essentials: chocolate, Coke, dinner.

Sadan was toilet-trained in so far as he knew when he needed to go, and he would squat where he was. Toilets were totally unfamiliar and there was no way he was going to sit on one of those! They were good only for entertainment, and he would flush it and laugh for a good half hour at a time. He was comfortable using a field or ditch but in the city it seemed the hotel or restaurant floor would do. After a couple of embarrassing incidents I put him in disposable nappies for the duration of our trip.

As he sat playing on our hotel room floor one hot Delhi afternoon, Alix and I heard Sadan talking. He hadn't spoken a word in the time he had been with us, so this was a special moment. I assumed he'd been quiet because of the stress of leaving the familiar orphanage and being placed in my care, and when I had mentioned his silence to a carer I was rather abruptly told he didn't have any problems.

As Sadan pushed his toy cars around the floor we could hear him talking to Madhu in long, excited sentences. Several months later, when Madhu had sufficient English to explain, we learned that Sadan had stopped speaking the day the boys were abandoned and had remained mute in the orphanage, despite Madhu's attempts to get him to talk. We recognised Sadan's speaking as a turning point at the time, but we didn't realise the pain that had held his voice silent for more than two years.

It was at this time Sadan decided he liked having a mum after all. He demanded to be carried everywhere, and would refuse to move if I didn't have him in my arms. I was grateful that he was such a tiny little mite. It felt lovely to be able to hold him as we spent our last days in India. Madhu stayed nearby but preferred to hold our Indian guide's hand when we were out. I told myself it was probably because he attracted less interest from passersby than he would holding a white woman's hand, but I longed for him to let me closer.

The boys were wonderful on the trip home. The excitement and novelty of flying was marred only by Sadan's total refusal to wear a seatbelt, and Madhu's 4 am air-sickness.

Once home they settled quickly. Madhu left the airport with his arm around his newly met Korean brother, Haden. It was instant mutual attraction. Madhu, with Haden in tow, walked around our home in amazement, opening the fridge and pantry, and turning on taps and drinking water that didn't need to be fetched from a pump or the river.

Madhu slept happily in his new room but Sadan refused any separation from me. He would only sleep on my bedroom floor so he could still see me in the lounge room in the evening. His terror at separation was easily understood, and he became my constant shadow for the next year. We nicknamed him 'the Klingon', as he was always clinging to one of my legs.

The boys surprised us all by quickly becoming two individuals within the family. We had expected them to remain a tight little unit within the family for some time, but Madhu immediately handed over all care of Sadan to his new dad and me. His trust was awe-inspiring. How could a young boy, abandoned by his parents and handed to strangers, trust so readily? At his introductory English class Madhu's teachers commented on his gentle nature and ready smile, and he won the hearts of all he met.

After some thought we decide on ages and birth dates, a new concept for children who didn't know how old they were. They each had their first-ever birthday party within a couple of months of arriving home. We had to show them how to unwrap presents and blow out birthday candles, but they got the idea quickly. Madhu suggested two birthday parties a year would be a good idea, to make up for all the birthdays he'd missed!

Sadan smothered me with affection and contact from the start. Madhu took much longer. At first he was resistant to affection and would reluctantly accept a quick kiss goodnight on his forehead, but only because I insisted.

A few months after we arrived home I was sitting on the sofa watching the evening news. Madhu turned to me with his arms spread apart and asked, 'Hug, Mummy?' I seemed calm while we shared a hug but my smile was a mile wide. At last I was able to hold my big boy in my arms. His hug dissolved all my fears that he might never allow me close. Madhu gave me a shy kiss on my cheek, and leapfrogged out to the kitchen. Less than a year later this same child jumped into our bed each morning and insisted on a ten-minute hug before he could face breakfast.

Madhu had an innocence that belied his life experiences. He had worked as a child labourer in a quarry for the early years of his life, breaking rocks with a sledgehammer and carrying them to a machine that crushed them into gravel. He still has the scars from accidents.

This child had known a hunger we had never experienced. One evening at dinner he told us in vivid detail how he used to catch wild birds and rats, then cook and eat them. The other kids sitting at the dinner table turned various shades of green. 'Why?' I asked stupidly. 'Because I was hungry,' Madhu explained.

One time the children were watching television and Madhu recognised Christopher Reeve from the *Superman* video they had seen. I told them about his riding accident and that he couldn't walk. 'He not fly either?' Madhu asked. The conversation became more confused when a clip of Elvis was shown. 'That man's a famous singer but he's dead now,' said Dad. A look of pure astonishment was on Madhu's face. 'If he dead how he move?' he asked.

Madhu brought home a poem he wrote at school on the computer. It was typed on a piece of paper cut in the shape of a heart. *Peace — by Madhu. Peace is not fighting and helping people. Don't cut trees. My Dad at night does work. I love my Dad and Mum.*

My little boys have borne so many losses. Their history, including all evidence of their first family, is irretrievable. With my help Madhu has written a life-story book to safeguard his memories and to assist his little brother who was too young to remember. No baby photos exist. We cannot tell them who they look like, or how tall they might grow. There is no knowledge of their real ages or birth names, save their first names, which Madhu knew and they have kept. Their birth parents and siblings are forever lost to them.

We were aware of the controversy of removing children from their birth country and culture for intercountry adoption. Children who have no say and who have already lost so much are taken from everything familiar to live in a foreign land with strangers. It is far from a perfect solution and should be considered only after any hope of restoring the child to their birth family or relatives is exhausted, and there is no permanent family or other suitable means of caring for them within their country.

Intercountry adoption continues to be the subject of impassioned debate but I believe we don't always separate out the issues of adoption from those of abandonment. Sadly, abandonment has all too frequently been the lived experience of our children – and any child who has lost his original family may well feel abandoned. Adoptive parents can provide love and security but we can't erase the pain of our children's original loss.

For my sons it was the only alternative to a childhood of institutionalisation, separation, and then, too young, being released on the streets alone. We cannot change this but we can give them a family, a place to belong, love and security, and we will help them rebuild a sense of their own identity.

Sadan no longer sleeps on our floor. He is now in his own bedroom but his little brown body is curled up to mine, fast asleep, every morning when I wake. He grew like a weed, making up two years' growth in the first seven months and increasing six shoe sizes in that first year!

Madhu's life-story book is special to us. The last page is written in his own words:

> I am happy in Australia. I like it because my house is good and I like having a fridge and good food. I like to go to school and play games on my computer at home. I like to do my chores and get pocket money. I like going to the shops and playing with Lego. I like my Mum and Dad. They are a good Mum and Dad. I am happy because they love me all the time.

Now, if I can only work out how to put all this into a few short sentences, then maybe I could answer that lady's question: *why would you want to do it?*

I wrote this story in 1996, the year after Madhu and Sadan became our sons. In 1998 I travelled back to India with 13-year-old Briony, and we brought home our youngest two children, Akil – then five years old – and his three-year-old sister, Sabila. Their adoption completed our family.

Madhu was aged maybe ten when he became our son, and he is now a young adult. In 2001 I travelled through India with him and he was able to see that his birth country was a magnificent place, filled with many generous people.

Sadan is now in high school. He has serious learning disabilities, but tries harder than any child I know. He frequently brings home merit and achievement awards. His teachers ring to tell us what a pleasure he is to teach. He is also a pleasure to parent.

Our boys came to our family as older children with unknown histories. We knew they were considered a 'risky' adoption. However, they have brought us more joy, love, and fulfilment than we could ever have imagined.

Madhu's story

Madhu Rollings

I'm Madhu and this is my story. I don't have a written history because I wasn't born in a hospital. I was born in a little village by a river, on a blanket in the hut that my family had built. I didn't have a birth certificate or baby photos, and nobody knows how big I was.

When my father left me and my baby brother at a railway station I was about eight years old, so I remember everything I went through. I felt very sad when I was thinking about why they abandoned me and I used to cry a lot. I used to cry every time I would think about it and it was very hard for me to look after my baby brother.

So when I was taken to an orphanage I didn't have anyone to help me know about myself and my family, and what had happened to us. I worried about what would be my future. I used to cry but nobody would come and talk to me, so I had to work out all these things by myself. I decided to try to forget about my past and my memories. It worked for a while because I had friends to play with, but then something would remind me and I would feel sad again.

When I was adopted by my Aussie family I was scared going with them because I thought they would leave me and do the same things that my other parents did, or do something horrible to me. The people in the orphanage didn't really explain who these people were, they just said this was my new family.

My life had to change again when I moved to Australia. I had to learn how to speak English and go to school. When I didn't understand English I used to think people were saying horrible things about me, about what a bad kid I was. I was scared because everyone was a different colour than me and I hadn't seen really white people before. I'd never used a toilet, or a bath or shower, and I'd never had enough to eat. Now I could get water easily by turning on a tap, and I could fill myself up when I was hungry.

After a while I learned how to speak English. My mum thought that because I didn't really understand everything that had happened to me – but I had a lot of memories – we should write a story book so that my life would start making some sense to me. Also so that my family would understand about my experiences and so that my baby brother Sadan would know what had happened to us in India.

So we used to sit down at the computer and I would try explaining to Mum some of my memories, and she would write them down for me. Lots of times she didn't really understand because I only had a bit of English and I couldn't think of the right words to tell her. Every few days we wrote the story, but sometimes I would get sad when we would write about a sad part. Sometimes I didn't want to write the book, so Mum would ask me to do just a little bit now and then. When we had written a page I would draw a picture on it about that part of my story. I liked doing the pictures more than writing the story because I didn't have to bother about English and the drawing part was fun.

When we finished the book, people in my family wanted to see it. Mum asked me if they could, to see how I felt about other people reading it and knowing about me. I would tell her if I felt comfortable about that.

I wanted to take my book to school and show it to my teacher because I felt proud about my book and I wanted my teacher to know more about me. After she read it she asked me if she could read it to my class. I said yes. The kids were good about it and nobody teased me about anything. They asked me a lot of questions about my experiences.

My book helped me because I could now get through thinking about my past without feeling sad each time I thought about things. Since we did it I am able to start talking about my birth family without crying.

Sometimes I get nervous talking to people about what has happened to me, about being a child labourer in India and being abandoned, and about everything else that had happened there. My friends want to know about my life, but sometimes I don't really know how to tell them. I let them read my book and ask me questions about my story, and I try explaining so that they understand me better.

I am still the same kid I was when I was younger. I still don't know how old I am, or when I was born. I still don't have any baby photos, as the youngest photo of me was taken at the police station after I was abandoned. Sometimes I think about what might have happened to my birth parents and brother and sister in India, because I don't know where they are or if they are okay. I know I probably won't get any more answers, but that is okay because I feel happy about myself and I understand more about what has happened to me. I'm glad about being adopted because I get love and attention instead of feeling miserable and thinking nobody loved me.

In November 2001 my mum and I spent a month touring my homeland. It was nearly seven years since I was in India and this was my first trip back. Had it changed since I lived there? I wanted to experience the culture and lifestyle. I thought I would remember lots of things in India and it would all be familiar, but I was wrong.

Before we got to India I was imagining how it was going to feel and what reaction Indians would have when they saw me with my mum, a white woman. The kids in the orphanage would remember me but what would they think of me? I didn't think much about my birth family because I knew I wouldn't find them or see them again. I don't really care how old I am because I've never known, so I didn't expect to find answers to that question on our trip.

India wasn't the same as I remembered. It all looked new to me because I'm now used to my life in Australia. We travelled heaps far, went through some villages, cities, towns and travelled all over the north. In the month we were travelling we went from Chennai in the south to Delhi in the north. We saw the Taj

Mahal in Agra, the Kama Sutra temples in Khajuraho, and we went down the river Ganges in a boat in Varanasi.

It felt like India had changed a lot because it wasn't the way I remembered it, but I know this is because I've grown up and my perception of things is different now.

I was really looking forward to going back to my orphanage and I was happy that I would see the kids who were there when I was. When we arrived things happened differently to how I imagined. The carers I knew weren't there any longer, and neither were the children I had known, so I was disappointed a bit but still happy to see my orphanage and the few girls and carers who remembered me. Boys have to leave the orphanage when they are about ten years old so all the older children were girls. There were still nearly 300 children in the orphanage but they weren't doing adoptions now so the children have to stay there.

I knew my way around but everything seemed smaller than I remembered because I had grown up. There were lots of babies sitting in cots and standing. The carers gave them biscuits to stop them crying during our visit. I was worried about the babies and how they were not looked after properly. There were only a few carers who just wiped the babies and were not loving them. The babies looked so sad and weak and skinny. I was sad that the children there wouldn't get adopted. I felt happy going back to visit but I am glad that I'm not there any more.

The worst parts of our trip were when people followed us everywhere and annoyed me with questions, trying to make us buy things. Also they were pushing and shoving on trains and buses. I found some things boring, like seeing too many temples. When we used transport such as the local bus or jeep I didn't like it either as it was uncomfortable. It was scary to look through the front windscreen at trucks and buses heading straight at us on single-lane roads.

This trip changed the way I felt about India. I found out that things were different to how I remembered them, and India was not all bad. Some parts were bad and need to change, like the poverty and the pollution, but lots of things were great. I learned so much more that I didn't know about my birth country.

I don't think of myself as being different than my white parents because I'm brown or because I am Asian. I'm not ashamed or sad about my past. I'm not disappointed that we didn't find my village or more about my birth family; what I care about is that we tried our best.

All I need to know is that my family loves me, cares for me and having been adopted by my new family makes me happy. I always feel happy because I have tons of friends and family who care about me. I have a very good education and am learning new things every day so I will have many skills for life. I feel that I now belong to both Australia and India. I am very pleased with how I turned out from all that happened to me and there's nothing that I want to change about myself.

My future isn't all planned yet and all I am sure I want to do is travel. I hope some day that I will get to go back to India and see if it has all changed. I can't decide yet what I want to be in life but maybe I will have to just try many things before I find the right one for me.

PS from Julia: Madhu has now graduated from college and started full-time work as an apprentice air-conditioning and refrigeration technician.

Angels are
forbidden here

Andrew Rate

There's a young father watching his children playing on the swings
and jungle gym on the green lawn of a suburban park in Perth,
Western Australia. The kids and their dad have no idea that a 30-
something man, watching the children play as he cycles past the
park on his way home from work, is finding it hard to blink
away tears of longing and anger.

I'm that cyclist; I'm hoping that the young family don't look
up and see my embarrassing response to their everyday family
outing. My grief is a starting point – shared with many couples –
for my adoption story, a story that is just beginning. As I write, my
wife and I have an application to adopt, and a stack of associated
documents in China, and we are waiting nervously to be allocated
a daughter.

We attended numerous information sessions and education
seminars, and tried to read as widely as we could on intercountry
adoption, and we often came up against the losses experienced
by adoptees and birth parents at the other corners of the adoption
'triangle'. We heard and read both positive experiences and
troubling stories which left us shedding a different kind of tears.
We had decided to apply to adopt from China, where we knew
potential adoptees are mostly abandoned girls. I was disturbed that
a Chinese girl abandoned at or near birth might grow up without
the stories that surrounded her birth and infancy. I know from my
own family stories and photographs that my father treated me like
glass when holding me for the first time, and that I was the
chubby cherub who crossed the equator with my parents on their
emigration from England to New Zealand. It's possible that such

stories may seem trivial to those not involved in their making, but my stories centre me and anchor me into a family, with all its associated history and eccentricities.

Prompted by the stories of loss of identity and culture, I wanted to create a story of origin for the abandoned child who would soon be living as a member of our family. The lack of concrete details meant that this story would have to be a plausible myth based on the shared stories of probably hundreds of children. Since our future daughter's abandonment would leave her without primal memories of her parents' love, or their later descriptions of her babyhood, the task I set myself seemed to be even more essential. The birth parents' loss, too, was something I couldn't get out of my head; perhaps my awareness of this loss was heightened by my mourning of the loss of my own potential biological children.

I doubt that I will ever understand the circumstances and pressures prompting parents, particularly mothers, to abandon a child to official care. As an affluent and comfortable citizen of a Western country it's far too easy to be judgemental, and the warnings about maintaining such a negative attitude as an adoptive parent were well taken. Anyway, I could not believe that such a desperate act could be carried out without the child's birth parents experiencing enormous regret and heartache. The cure for my discomfort was to include, in my imagined story of origin, absolution for the birth parents and through them, for myself for accepting their bittersweet and unintentional gift. The image of an abandoning mother, watching anxiously from the shadows until her daughter was found, was almost a throwaway comment in one of our information sessions. That image, though, was compelling enough to find its way into a poem, which at least helped me to shape a possible sequence of events in my own mind, and which I hope will be a starting point for many stories that I will tell my future daughter.

My first thoughts (and the first two verses) of the poem were for the abandoning mother who, in my imagined official sanctions against religious belief, had to act as her child's guardian angel. My attention shifted, and now stays with, the child who is the focus of much hope for us as a couple. During the tense waiting game that

She had harvest-moon eyes and
he was enchanted by them.
He carried a scythe in a muscled arm
and laughed like a mountain stream.
An afternoon's passion beneath the collective sky;
for two seasons, only
the terraced hills saw her swelling belly,
her creases of worry. In the spring
poverty and her family
were obliged to disapprove.
In the stillness before dawn,
three cries;
a rooster, a woman, and a child.

Angels are forbidden here
so she watches from
crisp morning shadow
across the dusty street
where, under the fading column
of characters of the police station,
in a cardboard box which once held
cabbages in the market square,
a tiny tassel of black hair shows
inside a precious woollen blanket;
she will be cold next winter.
A uniformed arm appears around
the opening station door;
from the streetscape's lone tree,
a plum blossom falls.

The tear on his cheek is
embarrassing but not unexpected.
Before, when someone else's
wrapped and basket-
borne daughter was
abandoned to official care,
the same salty emotion rose up and fell,
a rich and disturbing variation to procedure.

He will send for his wife;
she will know how to nourish the baby,
and who to speak to at the orphanage.
In the station porch,
a single bare light globe
flickers in its year-long glow.

The woman in the white tunic is kind
but she looks, sounds and smells
different depending on the time of day.
There is always
enough; first milk, now some solid food.
The infant learns to wait, but the waiting
fails to soothe her primal cries
for a constant and familiar embrace.
A tiny chamber of her inner heart
locks tight with a secret key;
a fleeting cast of dullness
darkens her bright sienna eyes.
In the swelling dusk
an aimless bright-sky bird sings
a stark lament to a waxing moon.

For three days the institutional air
has been tense with unease and expectation.
Doctors prod and measure; clothes are cleaned;
rumours of family and redemption
ooze and echo from newly polished floors.
Eight infant daughters of the revolution are
bundled into uncommon cars and more
than one nervous and regretful tear is shed
onto a bewildered child.
She has seen this once before; none of these children will return
and, for those remaining,
the added attention conceals traces of pity.
Sixty latitudes southwards, while
his wife sleeps, a sleepless man
waters a pot of white flowers.

substitutes for pregnancy, she is hourly in our thoughts and the focus of many prayers. I hope that the poem itself is a starting point for shaping an imagined history for our future daughter, a story to explain, to honour her family and culture of origin, to explore her beginnings with compassion and open eyes. At the very least it has helped me think about, and even go some way towards resolving, some of the doubts and tensions I had about the adoption process. Some of those doubts are questions about my own rights, if any, as an adoptive parent. On bad days, I wonder if the bleak description of institutional existence that I have written into the poem simply permits me, with a clear conscience, to offer our future daughter a better life. This thinking revisits the whole idea of absolution; as if any child is not a complete and gracious gift.

The sleepless man is, not surprisingly, me – again. Ever since I was a kid, I've had trouble sleeping, and it's hard now for my parents to take me for that hypnotic and surprisingly effective drive in the car. To be fair, the sleeplessness at the time I wrote the poem was more likely to have reflected worry about work, or some other mundane thing, than my concerns about the adoption process. I have the feeling, though, that all of my worries get mixed up with each other. It's hard, for example, to separate dissatisfaction with work from the ache of childlessness, because for me they're related at some level. For instance, I often feel, justifiably or not, that my work would be more bearable or fulfilling if I was supporting a family financially.

I'm looking forward to sleeplessness of a different kind. The novelty of being woken in the night by a young child is one I'm sure will wear off quickly, but at this point I'm saying, bring it on. Parts of me are bothered that I want a child so much – the part that is uncertain if we'll be successful in our application, and wants to protect me from the pain of disappointment, and the part that has listened to the officially sanctioned view that we're not to expect a child to make our lives more fulfilled or enjoyable. But I do want to have a child, in an innate and deeply ingrained part of my being! I love my friends' children and my nieces and nephews but, wonderful as they all are, I want more. The grief, the anger and the insomnia all suggest to me that my parenting instinct is bottled up inside; before the bottle explodes or the contents lose their flavour, I want to spend my fathering on my Chinese daughter.

PS: Andrew is delighted to be father to his daughter adopted from Anhui Province, China, in January 2005.

Loss and Grief

Through my mental haze I mumbled congratulations to my pregnant sister and tried to make all the suitable noises. Then I put down the phone and began to cry. Four hours later I was still crying.

Welcome a stranger

Katie Stewart

As one of six children, the thought that I might never have children didn't occur to me. I simply presumed that one day I would marry and have a large family. So when Peter and I married in our late twenties it was with the mutual dream of having three or four children. We were so confident that we put off trying for a year while we got used to being married. After that, we thought, we would soon be painting the spare room. The months came and went. We put it down to being older and told ourselves not to worry. After 12 months the visits to the gynaecologist began. Thermometers and charts became our timetable for life. Tests led to tests and more tests. Then exploratory surgery. No reason found, no cure discovered. The whole process became a chore. Life revolved around 'getting it right'.

Over time a small iron ball began to grow somewhere deep inside me. With each passing month it became bigger and bigger. Then it began to sprout spikes. For every newborn baby I saw, every pregnant teenager that passed me in the shopping centre, another spike would emerge. When there was no room for any more spikes the ball began to turn agonisingly. All the time I was putting on a brave face, smiling politely at the platitudes of friends and family, even when I felt like screaming. With three sisters all happily playing mother, family gatherings became a nightmare. My eldest sister had an inkling of what I was going through, having taken three years to fall pregnant herself. But, although caring and sympathetic, no one else seemed to have any real idea why I was so miserable. Look on the bright side, they said. Unlimited social life, nights without interruption, no dirty nappies or school fees. They couldn't understand that I would have given my right arm for all those things.

At last, after three long years, I found myself sitting in the room of my gynaecologist listening to his ultimatum. Either I went on the IVF program or I would never have children. It was as simple as that. He sat back in his chair as if waiting for me to eagerly grab at the opportunity.

'What about adoption?' I asked. He looked taken aback.

'Adoption?' he huffed. 'Adoption doesn't work!'

I tried to explain to him why I couldn't bring myself to go on IVF. I knew of people who had spent close to $70,000 trying to conceive a child. I could never live with myself knowing that I had spent that much money trying to make a 'child of my own' when there were already children in the world who needed homes. Nor could I deal with the idea of discarding unused embryos. Other people could do it if they liked. I wouldn't judge them. *But I couldn't.*

'What are you?' he muttered. 'Some sort of religious freak?'

'No,' I said, 'I'm just an Anglican.'

'Well go on and try to adopt then!' he said angrily, 'but don't come back crying to me in five years time when you're still childless. It will be too late then and it won't be my fault!'

'Don't worry,' I said as calmly as my anger would allow, 'I won't be coming back to you.'

Only a few days later, shortly after realising that, yet again, I had failed to conceive, my younger sister rang. She sounded embarrassed and was reluctant to tell me her news. Instinctively I knew what she was going to say long before she could bring herself to say it. She was having another baby, the second she had conceived in the time we had been trying for one! Immediately the spiky ball began to do somersaults.

'I didn't know you were trying,' I said.

'We weren't,' she said quietly, 'it was a happy accident.'

Through a mental haze I mumbled congratulations and tried to make all the suitable noises. Then I put down the phone and began to cry. Four hours later I was still crying. Self-indulgent? Probably. But three years of desperation, frustration and anger has to come out somehow. All the time I was telling God, to whom

I had prayed so often over those years, that he didn't exist. He was in fact a figment of my imagination and I didn't believe in him any more. It just wasn't fair! At last, exhausted, and with a quick apologetic prayer, I fell asleep in the arms of my worried husband. Through all my self-pitying tears I hadn't thought how he was hurting too.

The previous year had been spent planning my first art exhibition. I thought it would take my mind off 'things' and help me relax. The opening day was two weeks after my sister's phone call. Though I didn't sell out or make a huge profit I did make some money and had an enjoyable day into the bargain. I felt that at least I had found something at which I could be a success. My husband and I came home and celebrated with a bottle of Lambrusco. We felt more relaxed and happy than we had for a long time.

Shortly afterwards I plucked up the courage to visit my younger sister. We chatted the day away, carefully side-stepping any mention of the P word for as long as possible. As I was leaving she vanished to her bedroom and emerged carrying a pregnancy testing kit.

'I bought a double kit,' she said. 'Maybe if you use this one you'll get the same result.'

I told her how silly the idea was but I was touched by the thought. I took it with me when I left. Less than a month later I stared in disbelief at a blue line on that same tester. Was it my body spiting the gynaecologist, the effect of venting all that anger, or the efficacious properties of personal success and sparkling wine? Or had God simply heard me at last? I will never know, but nine months later I gave birth to a beautiful baby boy.

That's where the story should end isn't it? 'And they all lived happily ever after.' So why is this an adoption story? Unfortunately pregnancy was a never-to-be-repeated miracle. Primary infertility gave way to secondary infertility. The spiked, iron ball returned, this time with the added pain of guilt. On the one hand I felt guilty that I should be so ungrateful as to want another child when I had already been given such a beautiful son. On the other hand, I felt so inadequate not being able to provide that same beautiful son with a sibling. Again, no reason could be found. Again I was the cause of great disgust to gynaecologists. Adoption was not an option! How could I let my husband down like that? One doctor was so disgusted with me that, rather than explain the results of my tests to me, he proceeded to dictate a letter to my GP in front of me. In it he told him that I had no chance of having any more children and, as I refused to go onto the IVF program, he didn't want to see me again. My low opinion of gynaecologists was confirmed. Three years after the birth of our first son we started looking into adoption.

The decision to adopt came as a great relief to me. No longer was the onus on me to reproduce. I had begun to feel like a prize cow and looked forward to getting away from the prodding and poking, even if it did mean announcing my infertility to the wider world. Moreover my opposition to IVF had not been totally supported by Peter. He understood my reasons but did not entirely agree with them. It was a subject we tended to avoid. Agreeing to look into adoption was a big step for him.

However, if I thought that we had been through a stressful time up till then I was soon to learn what stress really meant. The first seminar we attended was so negative that we wondered if there was any point continuing. Overseas adoption, we were told, was expensive and slow. Local adoption was a much better option. We put down our names for local adoption but it soon became obvious that everyone who had been to the first seminar had done the same, as had all those at the seminar before. That meant about 80 couples waiting to adopt an average of five local babies a year. The odds were decidedly depressing. Peter, ever the pessimist (he calls it 'being realistic'), was ready to pull out altogether. Then we heard that there were not enough couples to fill the quota for Korea the following year. After much discussion we took our names off the local list and put them on the Korean list, but things still moved painfully slowly. After six months we were still no closer to assessment, though we had been told by someone in our support group that we should get into the next year's quota. In November, however, the rug was pulled from under our feet. Two other couples on the local list, both of whom had been waiting longer than us, had decided to change their preference to

Korea, meaning that we were no longer in the quota. Our wait would be another 12 months.

Again Peter felt that we should give up. It would never happen, and anyway, he added, we couldn't afford it. An hour later he changed his mind, but by this stage I too was beginning to think it was not worth the constant arguing. In desperation I went to visit our priest. He was one of those lovely people who says little but allows you to talk until you know the answer. I came away resolved once again to keep trying.

A few days later I saw him outside the church and he greeted me with a conspiratorial smile.

'Make sure you bring Peter to church on Sunday,' he said, 'and pay attention to the reading!'

I decided not to ask Peter to go to church. It would look too obvious. I got myself and our little boy ready and was surprised to find Peter dressed up too.

The reading was from Hebrews and began: *Welcome a stranger into your home, for he may turn out to be an angel.* And a little later: *. . . and do not worry about money.*

The reading had been set for that day years ago by someone who could know nothing of the significance it would have. Yet it said so much to us at just the right moment. After that there was no looking back. It was another 18 months before we were allocated a son, but we found the strength to go on. We waded through the red tape: the medicals, the assessment, the endless forms and bureaucratic garbage. We survived the stress of the Immigration Department losing the application papers for our allocated son. Four months short of three years after we put our names down for the first education seminar, we brought home our stranger, an angel with big brown eyes, black hair and enough energy to turn our world wonderfully upside down.

I would love to go back now to the doctor who told me that I would be letting my husband down by adopting, to tell him that after adopting our son we went on to adopt a beautiful daughter. It was Peter who made the suggestion that we should adopt again.

Now the family we dreamed of is complete. Maybe it didn't

happen the way we thought it would, or as quickly as we thought it would, but I no longer look on my infertility as a curse. Without it I would not have my three beautiful children. If I were given the chance to start my life again the way I wanted it to be, I wouldn't change a thing.

Except, perhaps, my gynaecologist!

A woman's wasteland

Wendy M. Anderson

Barren. Infertile. Sounds like a wasteland, doesn't it? Like a desert. Well that's how it feels when you're there. Yearning for a baby that doesn't exist is not like being a six-year-old who wishes for a pony each year when she blows out her birthday candles, then forgets about it until next year, or next falling star. It's like being the kid who is never picked on a team, who is left standing alone in the school-yard every lunch time. It feels empty and vast and inhospitable. And lonely. Very very lonely. At least that's how it felt for me.

Logically, I knew I was in that wasteland with my partner, someone I love dearly, the man who shares everything in my life. But in this, our sharing wasn't equal. I began to feel cheated, persecuted by remorse, plagued by black thoughts – he doesn't feel that aching need to be a mother. His stomach doesn't go cold nor his throat constrict with sorrow as hope dies again each month. He didn't even notice that there were six pregnant women in the supermarket this morning. I did.

Statistics may say that as many as one in four Australian couples will face infertility, but your eyes and common-sense say that one in four couples is not childless. When you are, it hurts.

A successful student, a successful career person, I had never failed to achieve anything I really set my heart and mind on. Except this. Except the one thing I wanted most in the world. And I was not in control of the situation. No matter how hard I worked, I couldn't make a difference. My efforts went without reward. It seemed so unfair. I felt alone, even though I knew I was not. Infertility knows no logic.

For over a decade, I persevered through barrages of drugs and exploratory and minor surgery. My partner and I endured perhaps a dozen attempts at various methods of in vitro fertilisation. The details and numbers are vague now, hazy, veiled by that quirk of nature that allows the memory of pain to become clouded. I was even pregnant a couple of times but never stayed that way for more than a couple of months. And I began to feel like a failure. Infertility affected my sense of self, stripped my confidence bare and banished me to the wasteland.

No clear reason for my inability to conceive was ever given. Pathological infertility they call it. I thought it made me sound like the problem was all in my head, like a pathological idiot. Like a fool. So I did a foolish thing. I began to build a wall around myself in that desert.

In the meantime, our friends were having families. Some were even complaining that a third child hadn't really been part of their plan. Childlessness was certainly not part of our plan.

I recall a dinner party where one of our guests – who had two beautiful children, a boy and then a girl – quite sincerely commented that at last she knew how I felt. They had been trying for a third pregnancy without result for three successive months. She was, she told me, very disappointed. I just smiled and swallowed the sorrow and anger I truly wanted to express.

There's a sort of social stigma attached to really discussing infertility. It's almost taboo. Like death, it's one of those topics that makes people nervous, uncomfortable. It gets tied up with religious concepts or ignorant prejudices, fear and guilt. So I found myself protecting the sensibilities of others at my expense.

Ironically though, as with pregnancy and child-rearing, everyone seems to have a quick word of unwanted advice. Try to relax. Get more exercise. Stop thinking about it. Change your diet. Take a holiday. Lose weight. Gain weight. Some even offered the explanation that my childlessness was like Darwin's theory of survival of the fittest, as if any fruit of my womb would be an aberration. Others said that it was God's will.

Some don't realise it, in fact many will vigorously deny it, but a sort of exclusionist superiority often goes with the myth of motherhood and the sorority house of bearing children. Childless women are frequently seen as selfish, or vain, or money hungry, or greedy for power, when in reality they are struggling to present a façade of success and happiness. Public identities so easily become caught up in the images we project. Personal truths run much deeper.

Many assumed that I had put my career, overseas travel and accruing of possessions ahead of having a family. They, of course, had selflessly sacrificed their business status, their financial independence, even their figures for their offspring. Their smug superiority cast me even further into the desert; made me want to build the fortress wall around me still higher.

Some women bemoaned their latest domestic drama – a sleepless night, a broken necklace, toast in the VCR – telling me that I was lucky not to have children. It took a long time before I had the confidence to look one in the eye and suggest, 'Want to swap?' She looked startled. 'Imagine, if you can, life without loving your children . . . Makes your chest ache, doesn't it?'

It should be remembered, especially by other women, that there is a vast chasm of difference between being childless by choice and suffering from infertility. Infertile women mourn the children they don't have. Monthly.

The condition of infertility should not be a lonely one. Person to person, there are things we can do to help the flowers bloom again in someone's desert. Cultivate conversation and nourish need. And to those out there in that barren place, take stock. Take heart. Look around. You are not alone. Be brave enough to share your pain. Be strong enough to ask for help. Don't build a wall around yourself. Rejoice in your talents and have pride in your achievements. Let your tears nourish your soul. Value the love that already surrounds you. And never, never lose hope. Cultivate even a small plot and the desert is not so vast.

Now, further down the track, I have learned to follow my own advice and I no longer dwell in the desolation. I am mother to two Korean-born children. There's a garden where the wasteland used to be.

But that's another story. I continue it in 'Out of the desert'.

Choices (Part 1)

Emma Caldwell

I had everything worked out when I was young. I was going to follow my chosen career until I found the 'one', then we were going to have children and live happily ever after. Oh how we set ourselves up for a fall . . .

Anthony and I met in 1980 when I was 17, he 19 and I, at least, knew I was going to marry him; the proverbial 'love at first sight'. We dated for a few months then started planning our future together. We thought we'd marry in a few years and we talked of children. We both wanted three or four but never took our discussions further – there was plenty of time for that. The day I turned 18 changed everything; I found out I was pregnant. Anthony and I had talked about marriage, had even become engaged, but a baby was not in our plans. Seven weeks later, Easter 1981, we married and in less than four months we had a son. Premature and tiny but ours and much loved. Our son, Jeremy, spent his first three months of life in hospital. He faced his share of struggles to live but finally he came home, still tiny but healthy and with a determination to be reckoned with. So began our happily ever after.

Our son was the most beautiful child in our eyes, with a beguiling smile and a cheeky nature. We were replete in our happiness. Some five months later I had my first miscarriage, our second son, but there was no official recognition of the birth – he was too early for that. We quietly named him and went on with life. While we grieved for our son it caused us no great worry as many pregnancies end in miscarriage and we were young with plenty of time to continue our family. We were busy enjoying

Jeremy and becoming more comfortable in our marriage. The next two years were so happy. We both revelled in our roles as parents, spending time with our son and giving no thought to more children. Jeremy was enough for now.

Then life decided we required more proof of its caprice. Our beautiful son somehow managed to get into a swimming pool one Christmas, and after 10 days of agony, watching, waiting, praying he'd be all right, he died lying quietly in my arms. I have never been able to see that time clearly in my mind, so much has been blocked out. But the pain we felt then has never left us, simply reduced in its intensity. Over the years Anthony and I have discussed that time and his recollections vary greatly from mine but both reflect the intensely personal nature of grief. I can't remember Anthony with me when Jeremy died and yet I know he was there. Anthony has similar blanks I'm sure. Proof that our minds do whatever is necessary to protect us.

A short time after Jeremy's death I found out I was pregnant again. The idea of having another child was sheer agony for me. I knew there was too much grief to be dealt with and I had nothing left to give another child at that time. I debated with myself over the possibility of an abortion but finally decided that I would have this child if it was meant to be. I miscarried several weeks later, another son – an end to my dilemma. In my naivety I believed another child would come into our lives when it was the right time. Our agony was compounded by the attitudes displayed by family and friends. While they all felt sad for the losses we had suffered none of them had a clue as to how to deal with it. They avoided mentioning our sons for fear of upsetting us; they would start to say something and stop suddenly or stop talking when we entered a room. There was a conspiracy of silence among those who were able to cope with seeing us. The others quietly drifted away, leaving us feeling unwanted and alienated.

Other people blithely thought they could imagine how we felt. None of them had a clue. It has always been my fervent wish that they never do. But we could not seem to make them understand that they had no true comprehension of what we were experiencing. There is simply nothing to compare to the utter devastation you feel when you lose your child. Losing a baby at any stage of a pregnancy is a horrendous ordeal. Most people see the likelihood of a new child coming into their lives as a dream and a hope yet to be realised. It helps to assuage their grief. But losing the child we had rocked to sleep at night, kissed better and laughed with took the misery ten steps further.

We spent the next few years dealing with the aftermath of losing our sons by hiding ourselves in any mind-numbing activity. During this time my doctors suggested I wait a few years before attempting another pregnancy and, despite various tests, were unable to provide a reason for my miscarriages or the babies' lack of growth. I could understand the reasoning behind the suggested wait, but found I was very angry with everything. I recall seeing pregnant women and shocking myself with the feelings this invoked. I was angry that they were pregnant. Who gave them permission? I felt anger, too, at people who treated their children badly. Angry with the sun for rising every morning, didn't it realise my child was dead? In my less irrational moments I could tell myself that allowing my body time to recuperate and my heart time to heal would help us to have a baby, and I could acknowledge that life would go on regardless of our private pain. But some things were incredibly difficult to face: shopping for gifts for other people's children or celebrating the birth of someone else's child.

I will never be able to forget the first Christmas after Jeremy's death. I had to shop for a gift for my only nephew (the others all came much later) and was unable to find anyone who could go shopping with me. I managed to find my way to a toy shop, tears streaming from my eyes and biting back sobs of grief. I left the store empty handed. I could not deliberately avoid children although anything that involved children caused me sadness. I sometimes vicariously enjoyed some benefits of being a mother through sharing time with other people's children. With a child in my arms again, I was the centre of someone's world for a few minutes and that took away some of the pain.

Incredibly, many people expressed their envy of what they perceived to be our situation. We appeared to have everything they wanted and lacked: the freedom to go where we liked, when we liked, and the financial resources to purchase what we wished.

They had children. It was a black comedy where everyone wanted what the other had, not realising the worth the other placed on what they had. The true wealth to my mind is a child, but many people appear not to appreciate that simple truth. If they have to lose a child to realise it, I hope they never do.

Finally we decided to start trying to get pregnant and so began the next stage of our lives. Getting pregnant wasn't overly difficult but staying pregnant was. I went through another four miscarriages over the next few years with no pregnancy progressing beyond 10 weeks. In 1990 I became pregnant for the eighth time. Three months later I was still pregnant but the baby's growth was poor. I had a cervical suture to overcome the possibility of an early delivery and several options were discussed aimed at assisting foetal growth. One of my sisters was pregnant as well; we were due within days of each other. As our pregnancies progressed it became obvious that my baby would be very small. Looking at a picture of the two of us at the time, my pregnancy was barely evident while my sister had a very noticeable bump. As I approached 28 weeks I began feeling unwell and finally, at 32 weeks, I was hospitalised. The doctors felt the only chance our baby had was to be delivered by an emergency caesarean section the next day. While nothing was said both Anthony and I knew our child had very little chance of surviving. I awoke from the general anaesthetic to be told I had a son. My doctor came and spoke to me and a short time later my husband appeared. As soon as I saw him I knew our son had died. Sam lived for two hours. Devastation struck us again.

A few months later my husband was transferred to a new job that required us to leave our home and move to the furthest corner of the state. I was not happy with the idea of leaving my family, particularly my new nephew who was the age Sam would have been. However, to my surprise, I soon discovered it was a good move and one that would ultimately bring us our child. We spent the next four or five years debating the wisdom of my getting pregnant. I endured another five miscarriages, all at less than 10 weeks. Then one morning I noticed an ad in the paper calling for expressions of interest in adoption. I pleaded, cajoled and begged my husband to consider the idea and he finally agreed;

the start of a long and demanding process. The idea of admitting we could not have children through the 'normal' means was scary, as was exposing our lives to strangers who we feared may judge us for the choices we had made. It's among the more difficult things I've had to do, opening up to those strangers: examining my motives for wanting a child and my commitment to becoming a mother – which would require giving up the freedoms I'd had available to me for so long – trying to decide if I had the capacity to love a child that held no biological ties to me, worrying I would compare a child to Jeremy, our perpetual angel. Memories of Jeremy were largely happy and any naughtiness had long been forgotten. On top of all of these issues was the fear that we would be refused access to adoption as I could fall pregnant and might not be considered infertile.

Even harder was coming to terms with the idea of 'taking' a child from someone else when I knew how hard it was to be a mother with no child. It felt like stealing to me. At the same time I felt anger at the idea a woman could voluntarily choose to give up her child. It was the most alien situation I'd ever experienced, desperately hoping that some woman would give me a child and therefore condemn herself to the agony I'd suffered. I still feel some guilt over this aspect of adoption and probably always will.

Through this period we started getting all the well-intentioned but ultimately stupid comments regarding our lack of children. With no real knowledge of our situation and no apparent concern for our feelings, people felt obliged to tell us to relax and 'it' would happen. Others preferred to advise that we didn't know what we were missing by having no children. I was pilloried by some for being a 'career woman', informed by others I was lucky to be childless and offered countless children so I could realise just how lucky I was. Many are the times that men offered their services as a substitute for Anthony, often in a joking manner but at times offensively. We received suggestions that I should spend the entire pregnancy in bed, to try faith healing, herbs, acupuncture, and a myriad of other 'sure-fire' solutions. Suggestions that we try IVF were just as unwelcome. For some reason people think they can comment on your reproductive ability with impunity and fail to grasp that, apart from being none of their business, it evokes such feelings of personal failure that their comments are like salt on a wound.

The amazing array of feelings elicited when investigating adoption still astounds me. Grief and anger, and the fear I felt in response to every question that our social worker asked – am I saying what they want to hear or am I shooting myself down? Am I really dealing with what went before or am I ignoring it? Do I really want a child or am I doing this because of some social expectation that marriage means children? Can I be a mother again or am I too selfish? Does it matter that a child won't be totally mine? Can I share a child with its birth parents? A million questions seemed to hit me every second and almost none of them ever got answered. Who knows how we'll feel, how we'll react until we get there. No one reacts in the same manner as another person, no one can predict how you'll be affected, not even yourself.

Slowly we found our way through all the interviews and completed all the paperwork. Nearly two years after commencing the process we gained approval to adopt a child. We had a 'licence' to be parents and now the really hard waiting would begin. We advised our families that we had been accepted into the program and could get a baby on very short notice. In an attempt to involve our families we started 'The Name Game' where anyone could suggest a name for our potential child. There were no prizes, only a baby for Anthony and me. It proved to be a hilarious way of easing the gathering tension. If we had followed the suggestions offered we could have had Heavenly Hirani Tigersnake, Belvedere, Rastus Mungo or perhaps Sunshine Buttercup. We encouraged the sublime and ridiculous from our families knowing full well that any child we had the honour of naming would provide the inspiration at the right time.

Little did we know that we were not going to be waiting much longer. Less than two months after being approved I received a phone call at work from our social worker. She wanted to speak to my husband and me at the same time so we organised that I go to my husband's work where they had a speaker phone. I spent the next 15 minutes convincing myself that she needed to speak to us about our smoking, which had almost cost us our chance to be approved. It was so soon there was no way it could be *the* call. We called the social worker back and she asked if we were both sitting down and could both hear. The speaker phone in fact wasn't working properly but we managed well enough. As I heard the words telling us there was a child whose birth parents had selected us I felt the most overwhelming joy I'd ever experienced. I was crying with happiness, jumping for joy and every other clichéd response you can think of – but for real. I couldn't breathe or speak for joy. As Anthony wrote down the small pieces of information we were being given my joy increased: a girl, a daughter for us; her name was beautiful (although we chose to give her a new name once we met her); she was healthy, nearly 11 weeks old and destined to be our child. The sun was shining on us again after so many years; suddenly all was right with my world.

To be continued in 'Choices (Part 2)'

In retrospect

Virginia Ruth Leigh

I was diagnosed with Turner syndrome when I was 12, in 1960. My mother and I received the information from our family doctor at his suburban surgery. Among other things, he explained that my short stature and failure to achieve puberty like my older sisters was caused by a genetic accident that occurred before my mother knew that she was pregnant. It also meant that I lacked, and would always lack, functioning ovaries. My one and only question to him was, 'I won't be able to have children, then?'

I had the extraordinary feeling that this matter would be very important indeed in years to come, and I needed to have a clear and unequivocal understanding of what I could expect. I was very young, even for a 12-year-old, yet I had a clear understanding of what I wanted out of life.

The doctor said that it did, indeed, mean that I would not be able to have children of my own, but that adoption would be a choice for me in the future. I simply filed the whole thing away, satisfied for the time being with what I had been told. Any emotional adjustments would come later, and I can see now that they did hit, as I headed into young adulthood. I expressed it through my attempts at writing, which were quite self-indulgent expressions of grief over love lost and unrequited. My mother, at the time of the diagnosis, probably felt the impact more than I did, but my parents were the type of people who, while loving and caring, always left me free to deal with my own situation in my own way. Perhaps their experience raising two other daughters, five and six years older than me, helped.

In 1968 I met Keith. Our immediate and total bonding took us both by surprise. As our courtship started to get serious, he raised the issue of children. We were both people who had very definite ideas of what we wanted, and no problems whatsoever in expressing our personal needs to each other. I also respected our relationship too much to leave him ignorant of important facts. So I told him of my situation and briefly explained why. The word adoption did not come up at all.

He didn't say much at the time, but he must have gone away and thought about it. He is the kind of man who responds to difficulties by saying, 'Okay, this particular path is blocked, let's investigate the alternatives.' The next time we met he brought along a newspaper clipping (from the *Sunday Mail*, of that very weekend, 18 May 1968) about all those babies waiting for loving families to adopt them at Adelaide's major maternity hospital.

Things were very different at that time. We applied as soon as we got back from our honeymoon, and our son was born exactly 40 weeks after our wedding date!

A short time ago I obtained a copy of that newspaper article. When we first read it, it simply encouraged us, letting us know that there were options available for us, choices that we were free to make. Reading it again now, it tells a most interesting story.

We lodged our first application for adoption in late 1969. This was before the introduction of the Supporting Parents Benefit in the 1970s. It was also during a brief period when the typical young woman having to decide what to do about her unplanned pregnancy was of the post-war baby-boomer generation, and the typical couple seeking to adopt was somewhat older. While the ratio of total births compared to births to single mothers had not changed, the number of couples wishing to adopt declined dramatically. There was a sudden oversupply of available babies and the worry for authorities was that they would have to expand their orphanages unless sufficient adopting families could be found. According to the article, the worry for the relinquishing mother was that an adoptive family would not be found and that her child would be institutionalised.

There was also potentially a greater demand on the homes for unmarried mothers because babies (and perhaps the mothers too) might have to stay there for up to 12 months while the new mums found accommodation and work to support themselves and their babies. The authorities were in a panic: where would they find the resources to cope with this? They needed adoptive parents.

Not long after this period, there was a complete turn-about in social attitudes to single motherhood, and government policy on welfare support had altered to reflect these changes before our youngest child was old enough for kindergarten. If we had waited a few years, it is quite likely that we would have missed out altogether. Waiting a while would have been a logical choice for us because, after all, I was only 21 when we married and we had nothing except my husband's job and some wedding presents, plus a little car that was only partly paid off and already starting to fall apart.

It is interesting, the understanding that comes later in life. I was very young to become an adopting mother. Most adopting parents today are in their thirties at the time of adoption, and have been married a few years. The female public servant who handled our adoptions terrified me – she was such a formidable old woman – good heavens, she must have been at least 37! At the time I thought she disapproved of me. As we walked into her office she probably thought, with horror, that we looked less mature than the relinquishing parents. Later I put it down to pressure of work on her part, and a slight touch of youthful paranoia on mine.

However, somehow we passed the test. In the middle of 1970 we received a phone call to say there was a baby boy available for us. We were living way out in the country at the time. Keith arranged immediate leave from work, we packed the car and off we went. We had no baby equipment or clothing because, somehow, we had not expected things to move so quickly. By next morning we were at the hospital meeting our baby and falling in love. Shopping for the necessities took up the rest of the day. Next morning we went to the hospital and reunited with our baby son, packed our car again, and off we went to start life as a family.

The arrival of our first baby was very sudden and unexpected. No doubt pregnancy is a time of anxieties, morning sickness and swollen ankles, but it is also a time when parents get to know their baby. It hasn't been born yet, but it is very definitely there. They have the chance to adjust. It was different for us; we were a child-less young couple one day and the next, a family. Adjustment took a little while.

I desperately wanted a second child, a daughter. There was always a longer wait for baby girls and while I waited I went through a period of terrible, helpless anger. The decision to have a child is a personal one between a man and a woman. The realisation that the intimidating woman in that dreadful government office had the job of making the decision for us was very painful. I realise now that I was grieving, and grieving deeply.

There was one sweetener. The local social worker at the time came and talked to us and inspected the house and the baby's room. He was a lovely man who became a close family friend. But while I had no problems with that particular social worker's role, I almost felt as though the staff of a whole government depart-ment, strangers who did not care, were in the bedroom with us. With the cost of both adoption and IVF these days, the bank manager may even be there, too! Then, when our son was just over two-and-a-half years old, we received the phone call informing us that there was a little girl available for us.

In 1996 I attended a gathering for Turner syndrome women and girls and their families. Cutting-edge reproductive technology was being discussed. A mother asked about the possibility of her ovarian tissue being taken and stored to assist her Turner syndrome daughter if and when she came to the stage of wishing for mother-hood. The woman who asked the question was in her mid thirties, and her ovarian tissue would soon no longer be viable for this technique. If she and her daughter were to take advantage of the future possibilities, she would need to have her tissue taken for storage as soon as possible.

I glanced at the woman's daughter sitting there beside her mother, listening quietly while this discussion was going on. She was the same age as I had been when I asked the doctor about my future prospects for motherhood.

My heart went out to her, for the very personal journey that she was just beginning. I understood that no one gets a road map for such a journey until it is at an end. I said a brief, silent prayer for her, and had the feeling that I had passed on a baton in some endless relay race. I felt a responsibility to do whatever I could, in my own small way, to be of support to people in her (or her mother's) situation. At the same time I felt a powerful sense of release.

In 1997 at the international Turner syndrome conference in England, there was a workshop on disclosure: who do we tell about our condition, how do we tell them, and when? A great range of people attended. Parents were wondering what to say about Turner syndrome to their daughters as they grew up, and how to say it. They were dealing with young girls who just love babies. They were also wondering how to explain to teachers if their daughters were, for instance, having the typical mild problems with maths or sport. Adolescents were wondering how to tell their friends, and how to deal with the prospect of dating. Girls a bit older were wondering what to say to potential suitors. The interaction between people at these various stages was tremendous and, for all of us, most valuable.

Towards the close of the conference, the mother of a teenage Turner syndrome girl was telling us how her daughter would not talk with her about it. I said to her, 'Let your daughter grieve. As long as you let her know that you are there – ready, willing and able to talk with her about it – and that you love her, she will come to you when she is ready.' That moment provided me with an insight into my own journey up to that point.

We introduced our son early in his childhood to his adoption story and its significance to our family. We discussed it briefly, when appropriate, as he grew up. He did not seem to have problems with it. However, to our surprise, being an adoptee became difficult for him as he headed into his late twenties. This did not seem to be anything to do with the relationship between him and us as his adoptive parents. Rather, it seemed to have arisen from the way adoption had become such a topical and emotional issue; at the time some awful stories were being presented in the media, in highly emotive language. Neither of our children could understand how different the economic situation and the social mind-set had been 30 years before.

While it seemed to be tougher for our daughter than our son during adolescence, the recent debate has not affected her so much because, as a mother herself, she has come to an understanding of the realities of parenthood. As a single mum, she needed to give her son emotional support during his pre-school years as he dealt with the pain of not having contact with his father. The other children gave him a hard time about it.

Then our daughter had contact with her birth mother. When the letter came from the government department saying that someone wished to contact her, her reaction was 'Mum, Dad, are you sure you won't be upset if I go through with this? You do understand, don't you, that she is not going to take your place?' She needed constant reassurance, even though we have tried consistently to let both of our children know that we felt no threat from their birth parents and that, while we would not interfere, we would understand and support them as they worked through, on their own terms, this most personal of matters.

It seems to be more difficult when the relationship between adopting parents and children is good, because the children feel that any natural curiosity or grief that they may experience is an expression of disloyalty to the parents who have raised them.

When our daughter met her birth mother (I'll call her Sarah), it was a disappointment to all concerned. She told me a few snippets of their conversation, and I was the one who had to point out gently, at the appropriate time, that certain things my daughter said might have been hurtful. I grieved for Sarah. On birthdays, Mother's Day and Father's Day, I have always said a little prayer for the people who gave our children life. I have understood all too well that relinquishing parents have powerful grief issues of their own to deal with.

My one hope is that future contact between birth mother and daughter will be more positive.

Two good things came out of the contact, however. Firstly, our daughter also met her half-sister, who is 13 months older than she is, and was also relinquished for adoption. She is also a young mother, and they have developed a significant, supportive relationship.

Secondly, it has helped our son. Health problems plagued him during his early twenties and sapped his self-confidence. I understand how devastating it is to find out when you are young that you are not bombproof. He recovered, and we are full of admiration for how he got his life back together. Because of his illness, he had to look to new career directions, and that took time and courage. The debate about adoption caught him at an emotionally vulnerable moment. But observing his sister's experiences seemed to help him resolve his own issues, and to come to some clear conclusions.

In a few days, Keith and I will be celebrating our 35th wedding anniversary. It will be quiet, just the two of us, no family gathering. We are an odd couple, somewhat surprised at the good time we have had over so many years, at the storms we have survived, at the way we have managed to accomplish what we needed to accomplish, without fuss or fanfare. To be human involves taking on unique challenges, and finding unique answers to those challenges.

Those affected by infertility go through the same passages in life as their sisters and brothers, but the path they take passes through a different landscape. As an older woman, I am quite grateful now for the challenges I have faced, because they have given me a focus on the important things in life – love, health, a sense of belonging and purpose – and taught me to value them as the precious, wonderful gifts they are.

My four sons

Lyne Moore

I dedicate this story to the memory of two little boys who entered my life for fleeting moments. They will remain in my heart for the rest of my life. And for the two little boys who are larger than life itself, who keep me going, breathing, laughing and loving every day. And last but not least, my husband. I love you and I thank you.

Like most young women, once I found the person I wanted to spend the rest of my life with, my mind eventually turned to the idea of having children. I had thought that I would get married, work for a couple of years, have a couple of children, be a stay-at-home mum and that would be that.

In the first year of our marriage my husband and I found out that we would have difficulty conceiving, even though we were not yet ready to have children. We later tried IVF and, sparing the detail, after two failed attempts we decided not to risk what might have been a considerable waste of money with little chance of success. Although we had briefly talked about adopting, we were a little sceptical. But I remember one night very clearly. While we were watching TV, Rick turned to me and said, 'Let's look into adopting a child.'

Our file left Australia in June 1998 for our first allocation. Exactly 12 weeks later Rick rang me at work. 'Hello,' he said when I reached the phone. 'You are a mum.' I must have let out a cry because my boss came running into my office to see what had happened. Rick kept repeating, 'But it's a boy.' We had requested a girl but said we would accept a boy if we were allocated one. It seems silly but the only reason we had requested a girl was that we could not decide on a boy's name!

In February 1999 we flew to Korea to bring home our first precious son. We had named him Dean. It is a day I will cherish for the rest of my life. We arrived at the adoption agency in the morning and introduced ourselves. We had not expected to meet our son on the day we arrived but our social worker, Miss Yoon, informed us that he was already there, being checked for a cold. We would be meeting him in five minutes. I went into a complete state of shock, unable to speak, worried that I would cry, wondering what I would do with no tissues on me. The first person I saw coming through the door was Mrs Lee, our son's foster mother. I could not see our son and as she approached I wondered where he was. Then Mrs Lee stood right in front of me and turned to the side. There he was, my boy, wrapped snugly on her back, in the traditional way the Koreans carry their babies. As soon as Mrs Lee took him off her back she handed him to me and I started to cry. Miss Yoon led us to an interview room where we spent about half an hour with Mrs Lee and our son.

Dean was seven months old and very aware of who his 'mother' was at that time. He kept putting his arms out to Mrs Lee. Mrs Lee would take him back and then turn him to face me, telling him *uhm-ma* – 'mummy' in Korean – and pointing to me. What a brave woman she was, coping with two complete strangers and a little boy so closely attached to her. She was willing to break her heart and let this boy call me mummy without any hesitation. Mrs Lee was a first-time foster mother so you can just imagine how hard this would have been for her. I have the rest of my life for Dean to call me mummy, I thought to myself, and she only has a few days left. Please let him keep calling you *uhm-ma*. Now when we talk about Mrs Lee, Dean calls her *uhm-ma Lee*.

Dean has added a dimension to our family that we never anticipated. He is a beautiful boy and I love him with all my heart and soul. He says his favourite thing to do with his mum is 'snuggling and cuddling'. I cannot seem to tell him enough times each day how much I love him. 'Me too' he always replies. And when he says 'Mum, I love you with all my heart', my heart still skips a beat.

After a year of parental leave, I returned to work in February 2000. Balancing motherhood and work was tiring. I remember crying at church one Sunday morning. A friend asked what was wrong. 'If I didn't know you any better I would have said you were pregnant,' she said. The next day at the doctor's I described my symptoms and asked for a thyroid function test as I thought my thyroid had gone haywire. The doctor suggested a pregnancy test. As I was coming back into his office I started to get a little shaky. What if I was pregnant? I tried to put it out of my mind. It was not possible; pregnancy did not happen to me.

'You are definitely pregnant,' the doctor announced within a few seconds of testing the sample. I was totally floored. I cannot remember a word he said after that except that he would like to confirm the result with an ultrasound the next day. 'What will my husband say?' I said to the receptionist. She knew our history and just giggled.

I rang Rick at work and told him that I could not remember how to get to him. He would have to stay on the phone and direct me all the way from the doctor's (only five minutes away in the real world). When I reached his street I saw him in the middle of the road flagging me down. Goodness knows what was going on in his mind. I stopped the car, got out and fell into his arms, blurting out that I was pregnant. He just looked at me with a strange, pale look of disbelief and didn't say a word. That same look remained on his face for about a week. The next day we went to the ultrasound clinic. Sure enough, there it was, a little heart beating away.

After the shock turned into reality, I had a fairly text-book pregnancy. One week in hospital for a kidney infection and 20 weeks of morning sickness but otherwise, no major complications. We went on with life expecting our baby to be born healthy, like any other parents expecting their second child.

At 39 weeks I was at my sister's house and my four-year-old niece asked if she could feel the baby move. I told her that the baby was sleeping at the moment and that when he woke up she could put her hand on my tummy and feel him move. I mentioned to my sister, a nurse, that the baby had been a bit quiet that day.

'Thank goodness,' I told her, 'because yesterday he was going crazy moving around and kicking, and then a bout of the hiccups at 10.30 at night.' At 39 weeks that was not much fun. After some time we decided to try to wake him up by poking at my tummy, but to no avail. By the time we reached home, 20 minutes away, he had still not made a move so I told Rick I would ring the hospital. The hospital suggested we keep trying to wake him and to come in if I was still concerned.

By 10.30 Dean was in bed asleep and Rick was winding down for the evening. I decided to drive myself to the hospital. The nurse had trouble finding the heart beat. I told her not to worry too much, that the baby was a little trickster. She said she would call in my obstetrician even though I felt it was too late at night. He arrived 10 minutes later and performed an ultrasound. Within a minute he had turned the machine off.

'I am sorry, but he is dead,' he said.

I was numb. The nurse asked if I wanted her to call my husband but I knew that I had to do it. When Rick arrived we just stood in the delivery suite holding each other and crying. After a while we decided we had better let our families know what had happened. My doctor induced me the next morning and after 12 hours of labour our second son, Luke, was born by natural delivery. Just before he was born the nurse asked if I would like to have the baby put on my tummy, or whether she should take him away.

'I don't know,' I said. But Luke was placed on my tummy while Rick cut the umbilical cord. I closed my eyes, too scared to look, but after a couple of seconds I opened them. Here was my second precious son. Then the nurse took him away to weigh and measure him.

On Luke's due date he was brought to our home for us to say our final goodbyes. We had bought him a white suit. We dressed him in our bedroom and held him for the last time in our arms and in our home. An autopsy was performed on our little boy. Everything was perfect; there was no explanation for his death. It was just one of those things that happen.

I have a little gold heart that I have always worn around my neck. My mother bought it for me when I was about 19. It has the letter L engraved on it for my name. Now the little heart I wear around my neck with the letter L is for Luke, the little boy who entered our lives for such a short time and who will live in my heart forever. Luke is and will always remain an integral part of our lives. He has helped to shape our family into the people that we are today.

We had already applied to adopt again before my surprise pregnancy and a year after Luke's death we decided to continue with the process. I received the telephone call that we all wait for in February 2003. Another boy! We were overjoyed. We had narrowed the choice of names down to two and we let Dean decide which he would prefer for his brother. So Joel it was.

Who says you don't bond with the photo? The entire family did. To us adoption was guaranteed and nothing was going to hold us back. We had lodged our immigration papers, completed the affidavits, paid the adoption fee and everything was set to go. All we needed was approval to travel.

I arrived home from work one Thursday afternoon to find a message on the answering machine from the department asking if I could call them back. We did not think too much of it. I rang the department in the morning. Joel had been in hospital and the Korean adoption agency had sent across medical and lab reports. The social worker read me the reports. She did not think it sounded serious and suggested it might be eczema. I was distressed; no parent likes to be told by a non-medical person what may be wrong with their child. I rang Rick and then made an appointment with our paediatrician, hoping for reassurance. In his office we asked what he thought was indicated in the reports and what the worst-case scenario might be.

He told us that the reports didn't look too bad; quite often young babies could have these results followed by a normal result when retested. He was, however, concerned about the shape of

Joel's head. He explained it could be anything from epilepsy to cerebral palsy and gave us a list of tests that should be carried out on Joel, tests that would be at the overseas agency's discretion. By the time we left his office we feared that once again we would be saying goodbye to a little boy who, for a fleeting moment, had joined our family.

When I finally got to work that morning I rang the social worker about the visit to our paediatrician and our uncertainty about what to do. 'Let me know what you decide,' she said. I felt unsupported.

After a restless night and lots of tears we advised the department the following day that we could not proceed with the adoption. We wrote a letter to the adoption agency in Korea advising them that it was with great regret and heartache that we would not be in a position to adopt Joel on the information provided to us and after discussions with our paediatrician.

A few weeks later I received a call from the department advising that the overseas agency had carried out further tests which had confirmed our paediatrician's suspicions. When I quizzed the department for details they said the overseas agency would not tell them as they had to protect Joel's interests if he was placed for adoption again. Our file was placed back in the allocation pool with the overseas agency. I was anxious. Had we done the right thing? What if it all went wrong again? What if, what if, what if?

In June 2003 while at work I listened to another phone message from the social worker. I returned her call and was advised that we had been allocated yet another boy. There was no real excitement. I requested the facts in a monotone voice and told the social worker that I would come in the next day to get the paperwork. I rang Rick, even then still not wanting to get too excited. I told him that we had been allocated a boy. Four boys – who would have believed it? We received a photo about a week later and slowly I started to attach, but held back until Carl's medical had been approved. We did not want to tell Dean anything about Carl until we were 100 per cent sure that he was coming home.

It has been nine weeks since we were allocated Carl and today we received news that our son is ready to come home. I have been jumping up and down on the spot in disbelief! We have three days to organise everything before flying out. We are in the middle of home extensions and renovations, believing we had a couple more weeks for painting and carpet installation. Instead we will be leaving our home in chaos. But who cares . . .our son is coming home!

Hope

Perhaps all the years of infertility treatment and then the tortures of the adoption process just added up to a perverse desire not to be beaten by something.

Letter to my son's mother

Claire Laishley

The last balloon has burst, the last chocolate has been ground into the carpet and all the guests have departed. Most of the presents have been put away for a rainy day and the house is peaceful once again, after two hours of chaos.

You've been with me in thought so much today, the day our boy turned two. How proud you would have been of him. I know I was. Like the other children, he ate too much, became over-excited and cried when things didn't go his way.

He's always been such a beautiful-looking child, with his navy-blue eyes, fair curls and cherubic face. But the inner child is just as delightful. His sweet nature and incredible affection are a constant source of joy to our family. I know this warmth could only come from a woman who was once asked to make the biggest decision of her life, entrusting her child to another. And would you have been so trusting, I wonder, if you'd realised how ill-prepared we were to receive this new addition to our family?

I look back on that period as my 23-hour pregnancy. It was the late 1970s; I had been married for six years and had a successful career. My boss was travelling interstate two days later and I would be in charge of the office. I was confident of my ability to run things smoothly in his absence and had covered all bases – except one. I could not have anticipated the phone call that came through on the Monday afternoon at 4 pm telling me that a two-week-old baby boy was waiting at the hospital for us.

'Could you pick him up at three tomorrow?' the voice asked.

My husband and I had constantly been told not to get our hopes up. The department couldn't guarantee an adoption for us so we were to carry on with our lives as a couple and not hold any expectations of becoming a family. I was the only female working in a small architectural practice, and while it was fun to play 'mother' to my boys, I sometimes thought this might be the only maternal role I would ever experience.

It had been at work that I had confronted the worst day of my life. Two years earlier I received a phone call that would send me into the depths of depression.

'I'm so sorry,' the family GP said quietly, 'the test results are not good.'

There was a pause as I searched my mind for an appropriate response but the doctor, picking up on my discomfort, quickly continued, 'There is no trace of active sperm.' I'd read many articles on fertility but somehow misinterpreted his words. When I started to explain to the doctor he cut in.

'I'm sorry but it's not just a low sperm count, there are no active sperm at all,' he repeated carefully.

Those last seven words echoed down the phone line but only one thought kept hammering in my brain. How dreadful for a doctor to have to make this sort of phone call. It was much easier to concentrate on someone else's problem. Ten minutes after hanging up I was still staring at the phone when the awful reality suddenly penetrated the fog. There would be no children. We would stay a couple, growing old, just the two of us. No first day at school, no one to call me 'Mummy', no high school graduation, no grandchildren.

I pushed my chair away from the desk and ran into the kitchen. I felt trapped, unable to face any of my co-workers, and as I stood clutching the sink the tears flowed and turned into deep sobs. I was vaguely aware of the conversation filtering through from the drafting office but I was beyond control.

'Is everything all right? Anything we can do?' one brave soul enquired.

I quickly wiped my eyes and turned, feeling the hint of a smile pushing its way through my despair. My boys had obviously felt this was too great a task for just one of them and so they all stood, hesitantly hovering. As much as I needed to share my feelings with someone at that moment, I knew it was too much to place on them. How could they even begin to understand what this means to a woman? I assured them I would be all right, just needed a bit of time alone. The cumulative sigh of relief was audible.

The next few months were extremely difficult for us as we struggled to come to terms with this body blow. We eventually decided to put our names down on the adoption register, and spent the next two years full of guarded hope.

And now, another phone call and I was experiencing the opposite emotion. I can still see the look on my boss's face as I ran into his office and announced dramatically, 'I've just become a mother!' As the news filtered through the office, the boys were relaxed enough this time to approach me individually; happy news they could handle.

But when I arrived home that night and the excitement started to abate, the reality of the situation hit me like a bucket of cold water. I wondered if the feeling of nausea I experienced was an adoptive parent's version of morning sickness. Apart from a dozen disposable nappies, two plastic bottles and a spare room with little spare room, I had nothing prepared.

I had promised the boss that I would go into work the next morning and tidy up some loose ends, so had to rely on relatives and friends to organise things on the baby front. When I arrived home at 1 pm, my emotions were close to the surface once again. My mother had created a nursery from 'no spare room' and the washing line was crammed with rows of tiny clothes.

There were so many mixed emotions as we drove towards the hospital that day. I felt as though I'd been thrust into an acting role but someone had forgotten to tell me the plot. We walked into the maternity section of the hospital and the matron placed a small bundle in my arms, the most beautiful baby I'd ever seen.

The first night home became a daze of visitors, anxious to welcome our new family member. I was on automatic pilot; there was just too much going on, and I was finding it hard to adjust to this interruption in my well-ordered life. I wasn't excited anymore, just terrified. What made me think I could be responsible for another human being?

Thankfully, the front doorbell eventually stopped ringing and the last guests left. I just had enough energy to settle the baby down and crawl into bed. It seemed only minutes later that I was woken by a strange noise, and realised it was feeding time. I sat in the lounge chair gazing down at the small mouth sucking hungrily on the teat – and fell in love. I started shaking, it was so unexpected. I'd read all the books about the importance of those first moments just after the birth and the bonding process that occurred. I didn't have an opportunity to experience that and I'd tortured myself with impossible questions. What happens if I don't like the baby? How long does it take for love to grow between mother and adopted child? But miraculously, that night, I had all the answers. I brushed my hand over the fair curls and made our boy a promise that I would always love and care for him.

I was scared to let my thoughts dwell on you too much. This baby was mine and no one must come between us. But then I remembered we still had to endure a period of three weeks when you could reverse your decision about relinquishing your baby.

Twenty-one days, somehow it became easier if I could mark my mental calendar in that way. Each morning as I walked into the nursery and looked at the baby, I'd steel myself from wondering if this was the last day we'd spend together. I cursed a group of faceless people sitting in a government department holding sway over my emotions and our future.

Some days I found myself performing the routine associated with a newborn infant with an almost cold detachment, telling myself I was merely a long-term baby sitter. But I hadn't allowed for the fact that I'd fallen in love and, as at the beginning of any relationship, I wanted to embrace everything about that other person. How would this attitude affect my relationship with my son in the early bonding weeks should you, his mother, keep to your original decision and allow this baby to became part of our family for ever?

As well as my own growing attachment, I had to warn the extended family and friends this may only be a temporary arrangement. I felt an almost manic need to curb their enthusiasm, but was constantly told I mustn't concentrate on the negatives.

Several of my friends were new mothers, too, and I couldn't help wondering, bitterly, how they would react if they knew there was some faceless person hovering in the background, waiting to ruin their lives.

About two weeks into the waiting period – on the thirteenth day actually – my mother phoned to say she'd be calling in with a friend. This friend's daughter had given birth to a baby the day before mine and the proud grandmothers were anxious to compare their new grandchildren.

I remember thinking it a little strange. Mum had lost contact with this friend a few years before and suddenly here she was, turning up out of the blue. As we sat in my lounge room discussing the additions to our families I experienced a stab of pain in my chest.

'Do you realise our babies were born at the same hospital?' the new mother asked. The pain around my heart intensified and a wave of nausea struck. I sent a desperate look in my mother's direction, begging her to take these people away. Couldn't she read the fear on my face? I knew immediately that being a small private hospital, this woman would have met you, would know what you looked like, and as we sat conducting our civilised conversation she was probably taking mental notes to pass on to you later. I stood up clutching the baby to my chest, his small face hidden against my shoulder.

'You have to go now,' I stammered. 'He needs an afternoon nap.'

My mother still hadn't picked up on my anxiety and looked horrified at my rude dismissal. After I closed the front door, not even bothering with goodbyes, I sat and rocked my baby and the tears flowed.

The next day dawned and I woke with an even heavier heart. Before I went into the nursery, there was one phone call I had to make.

'How could you do that, Mum?' I sobbed. 'What were you thinking?'

My mother was distraught; she had failed to sense the significance of the situation. 'Oh darling, I'm so terribly sorry. I didn't think.' We made our peace a few days later because I soon realised

I needed my mother; someone experienced who had shown joy and acceptance of this new family member.

It was the final day of the three-week wait. This would be the last opportunity for you to change your mind and if this happened the department would phone to inform us. I wasn't prepared to lose my son at the last minute. Thankfully answering machines and mobile phones were the technological future, so all I needed to do was to leave the house. I packed the baby bag with bottles and nappies and was out of contact by 8.30 am.

Somehow the hours of that day passed and at 5 pm I felt confident enough to return home. I settled my son—yes my son—in the bassinet, knowing we were safe. I felt the love that I'd been trying to quash for the past few weeks completely overwhelm me.

I looked at my perfect child and for the first time I allowed myself to wonder what you looked like. I realised I wasn't the only one who'd gone to hell and back over the preceding three weeks. Had you wrestled with your conscience over those 21 days, or were you confident in your original decision? I will never know, but from that moment, my feelings of fear were replaced by feelings of gratitude.

I wrote this two years after the adoption was formalised and I remember that moment when I was able to relinquish the fear that someone would take my baby away. Each birthday since, I have looked into my beautiful boy's eyes and silently sent thanks and love to my son's mother.

Out of the desert

Wendy M. Anderson

ART (Assisted Reproductive Technology) always strikes me as such an ironic acronym for something that can be so utterly clinical, so totally without soul.

It had been a long time since our last active cycle of ART. We had decided to take a break, to get on with the life we'd put on hold – to travel, to play. I wanted to commit to my career so that I could once again enjoy the self-confidence that holds my right hand whenever success holds my left. I wanted to feel whole. I needed weeks and months and years to pass without having to count days, have blood tests, inject myself, ride the crests of hope and weather the troughs of despair.

Remarkable stresses are associated with undergoing ART – physical, emotional and financial – and while many couples find that the experience binds them irreversibly, many more begin to drift apart. Countless marriages don't survive and ours had begun to show signs of strain.

Despite each couple having one specialist to oversee treatment, it was possible, in the program we undertook, to have every step of the procedure performed by a different member of the IVF team. Sometimes we saw three or four different doctors in a week, none of them my choice. None of them knew us or the story that made us unique. We felt like statistics. It was time to stop.

So I changed direction. I moved into a new and challenging job. I made new friends. We worked on our marriage. And we left the last batch of frozen embryos to wait. We dubbed them The Cryogenic Carltons (my married name) and made jokes about having the super-race on ice.

Back then, counselling was mandatory for all couples on the infertility treatment merry-go-round. One session of it. One hour of counselling before undertaking that journey into the wasteland. More was available, but we were never invited to use it. No one suggested it may be time to get off that mad carousel, they merely encouraged us to try a different horse, or another tune, put another coin in the slot and go around again.

No one spoke to us of the possibilities for happiness in a child-less marriage, or of alternative roads to parenting. We were unaware of the waiting lists and the age requirements for local adoption. We had no idea what was involved in fostering a child or what permanent care meant. The newsletters from the IVF support group we had joined seemed to be full of the success stories of others, or advertisements for meetings of the sub-groups – like the one for people whose babies had died. Maybe I wasn't listening, but there just didn't seem to be a voice speaking to us. There was no middle ground.

Then one day, unexpectedly, a familiar voice reached me. It was my mother's. She walked into our home one Friday night and placed a small, neatly clipped square of newspaper on the family-room table. It was an advertisement for an information night to be held by the state intercountry adoption services.

A phone call plus an information night and our lives were changed forever. It didn't matter that we were almost 40. It didn't matter that I was infertile. There were still rocks to be climbed – the process would not be quick or cheap – but we were assured that if we stuck it out, at the end of the journey there would be a child.

So we began to traverse another wasteland, leaping from rock to rock: education groups to warn us of the problems and discuss the issues associated with parenting a child born in another culture; medical checks; financial checks; police checks; four written references from friends and family members declaring that we would make suitable parents; answering some 200 questions about our appearance, personalities, backgrounds, courtship, sex life, faith and attitudes – in writing; producing a family tree; visiting families with children adopted from overseas;

meeting members of the communities of migrants from the various countries from which it is possible to adopt. We even had to do a project, just like we used to do in primary school, to demonstrate that we had some knowledge of the country from which we had finally chosen to adopt.

Then came the home visits from a social worker to check out what we'd written about ourselves and conduct a safety audit of our home. Her task was to decide whether we were suitable parent-material. In our first lives, both my partner and I were teachers. Ironically, the young woman assigned to us had recently married one of our ex-students; now here she was writing a detailed report card on us.

We wanted our baby to be as young as possible and, among the countries whose orphans and relinquished children are acceptable to our government, Korean adoptees are generally the youngest to arrive in Australia. At the time, around 16 South Korean babies, mostly under six months old, were being allocated for adoption by families in our state each year. So we knew that in our year's batch, there would be other like-minded families for us to befriend, other Korean adoptees to grow up beside our child. That was important to us. Families with children who do not look like their parents are both the same as and different from other families. It's helpful sometimes to be with others who understand entirely.

Eventually we were declared acceptable potential parents – and then came the paperwork specific to Korea. Then, the wait.

Waiting to be approved and then allocated is a long, challenging and intrusive process but for us, after the indignities of ART, it was never really painful. That exhaustive series of checks and cheques was both draining and frustrating, but this time it was certainty rather than hope that kept us going. We were confident, at last, that at the other side of the desert was our child. All we had to do was jump through the hoops ... and wait. And this time we could do all the travelling together, my partner and I. Everything that happened, every intrusive question, every uncomfortable procedure, was performed on us both, not just me.

We had to bite our tongues when people with biological families pontificated about how appropriate it is that the adoption process should be so complicated. Easy to say when your decision to have a family was made in the privacy of your own relationship. Easy words to mouth when no one is scrutinising your life, your feelings, your thoughts. Now, years after the process, I can agree with them – but for reasons different from theirs. All parenting requires perseverance, patience, faith. Parenting adopted children has added challenges.

You see I don't believe that being fertile should come with the automatic right to have children. Having children is a privilege that too many people abuse. But saying so tends to offend or invite empty agreement from people who have never considered parenting in that light. And if parenting is a privilege, there is no greater privilege than being chosen to parent someone else's child. And doing so is complicated. Very.

Just to make sure I didn't become too complacent during the anxious wait for allocation, it became obvious that one potential base cause of my infertility, my endometriosis, could no longer be either treated or ignored. The only course of action was a radical hysterectomy. So back to hospital I went and I must admit, there was a strong element of relief amidst the many other emotions coursing through me.

Just a week after the surgery, as I lay uncomfortably on the couch staring blankly at the horror that is daytime television, our social worker phoned. She was going to bring us two small photos of a baby boy who was six weeks of age and as much information about his birth parents as was available. We had 24 hours to decide if we wanted him.

It took about a millisecond.

It's hard to explain to others how it feels to become so attached to a photo of a child you haven't met; that you keep copies of it all over the house, in your wallet and even sleep with it. For the next 12 weeks, while yet another batch of documents was completed both in Australia and in Korea, those photos of our son were all we had.

The baby had to pass health tests and be issued with a Korean passport. When an Australian adopts a child from overseas, the process cannot be finalised until the child has become an Australian citizen. For that to happen, the child must be a resident for over a year. Before that, he or she is technically and legally considered to be under state care. So for the first year, our child's passport and medical records were all kept under his Korean name, not the name we gave him. During that year, more checks and reports are done. At the end of that year there is another set, the final word. Only after that can you proceed to finalise the adoption.

So it was nearly three months after we saw and fell in love with our small photo of Jong Koo that we took off for Seoul to meet our son. In Korea, babies destined for intercountry adoption are fostered. In one photo, our little boy was propped up on his foster mother's lap. After that we had no further information about his development, or pictures of him, but we knew he was being cared for and loved in a family environment.

His remarkable birth mother had relinquished her illegitimate son so that he could have the sort of safe and comfortable life she knew she could not give him. His remarkable foster mother had carried Jong Koo in a sling and slept beside him for three months, fed him when he cried, nursed and nourished him. Now, unremarkable James and Wendy were going to take him from her and bring him back to Australia to be Finn Andrew Jong-Koo Carlton. We felt humble as we wondered if we would even recognise him.

There was absolutely no mistaking either Jong Koo or his foster mother. We knew them the instant we set eyes on them that hot day in the adoption office in Seoul. Anxious for the baby to make a good impression, the foster mothers are often reluctant to hand their small charges over to the crying strangers, the overwhelmed new parents. They don't want the babies to cry too. And that first meeting lasts only an hour or so. It's like having an interview with your new son or daughter, just enough time to check each other out. Then the baby returns home with its foster mother for the next few days until yet more documents are completed.

Most Australians who adopt from Korea collect their child from the adoption agency the day that they fly out. Just hours before their scheduled flight, they go and collect a baby sling, a change of clothes, a bottle, a small tin of formula ... and their baby. Then they board a mini-bus that takes the new family to the airport. For these new parents, the first real experience with their baby is an international flight. It's nerve-racking.

We were honoured to have been invited to collect Jong Koo from his foster family's home the day before our return flight. His foster mother had asked all the neighbours, who knew and loved him, to meet us and to say goodbye. She had also organised for the family priest to come and bless the baby for his life in Australia. She had prepared a small banquet of fruit and cakes. Her kindness was palpable. Just as she had welcomed Jong Koo into her home and family, so too she welcomed us.

His tearful foster mother showed me how Jong Koo liked to be held. The social worker translated for her as she told me when he cried and how often he took a bottle. Then she handed me a small album full of photos of my son's first four months of life, the part in South Korea—the part I had missed. And we both wept.

Already this small boy was loved by three mothers. I am lucky number three.

At journey's end, I can honestly say that I had to traverse that wasteland my own difficult way. I had to give ART my best shot. I had to take my own time to realise that what I longed for was a child, not a pregnancy. Mothering means so very much more than giving birth. Being a family is not easy. It should never be taken for granted.

I feel sorry for those who mistakenly believe that their children are extensions of themselves. Or worse still, those who are so wrapped up in themselves that they can't imagine loving a child who is not made in their own image.

And I have a ready response to all those who say to me: *Well, you did it the easy way, didn't you? You didn't have to go through the pain of childbirth.* I reply: *I suffered my own pain—a hysterectomy was a very minor part of that pain. And I had to miss the first 20 weeks of my son's life. Would you really trade your child's first months to avoid giving birth?*

But as for childbirth, time and love conspire to dissolve the memory of pain. So you do it all again. Finn now has a little sister, Lara, born Ha-Yeong. She is the rose beside her brother, the towering sunflower in the garden of our family.

PS: We love being flowers for Mummy and think this story should be called 'The Sunflower and the Rose'. F aged 7 and L aged 4.

Hope

Elisha Barrow

My husband and I had talked about adoption but didn't really know what was involved. All we dreamed about was the end of the journey: a child and a family. My first enquiry was with a counsellor. She seemed to know a lot about adoption. She told me there were a lot of babies being adopted from Korea and the process only took about 18 months. I was really excited about this. The counsellor advised us to go and talk to the local adoption agency to find out more. We booked an appointment. We had already decided that to adopt a child was what we wanted and we just needed to find out how.

I had just turned 23 and my husband was 41. The age restrictions meant that we could adopt a child no more than 40 years younger than my husband. Though I was a lot younger this didn't count for anything as the age difference was calculated from the oldest in each couple. If we adopted a second child there could be a 45-year age difference between the child and my husband, so there was a chance to have a younger child down the track. The other restriction was my age. The minimum age to adopt a child was 25 years.

We were disappointed that we wouldn't be able to adopt a baby but quickly accepted the possibility of having an older child.

We started the process in 1998. We went through most of the paperwork slowly. The fact that we still had a few years to wait before I turned 25 meant that there was no need to rush, no pressure. If we had fully appreciated the extent of the paperwork we would have worked faster.

We hadn't told anyone of our plans to adopt, not even our close family or friends. This was my choice as I didn't want people constantly asking how things were going. We passed little comment about having a family and if asked we responded vaguely. When we had to get references we realised that the time had come to tell at least two people. We decided to start with our families.

My husband and I have always had a close relationship with my parents. They live close by and in the early years of our relationship we both lived with them. I have a sister who is 10 years older than me. She has children but lives in the UK so my parents don't get the joys of being hands-on grandparents. I was well aware that they might initially experience loss, with us not having biological children. I was nervous about telling them but deep down I knew that everything would be fine. We invited them to dinner, after which we told them of our plans. I can't remember the details of the conversation but they left soon after our announcement. As I expected, it shocked them. My husband and I knew that they would just need time to let it sink in.

The next day my dad popped in and asked which room we would have as the child's bedroom. It was his way of starting a conversation about adoption. He wanted to know how long until we were allocated a child, how old it would be, and whether a boy or a girl. A few days later when I saw my mum, she started talking about clothes and toys for the new child. My parents have always been happy with what I have wanted from life and accepted my decisions, so I never doubted their support this time.

My husband's family live interstate. They accepted the news positively. My mother-in-law was especially excited. I think having children was something that she had always wanted for her son.

We were relieved once we had told our relatives. We could discuss things with them, and they could travel on our journey with us.

We had chosen India as our preferred country of adoption. The program was running smoothly and the children were the right age for us. Other countries had restrictions regarding religion and the length of time the parents had been married. Like most other adopting couples, we wanted a child as quickly as possible.

Collating the information required for our file for India was time consuming. We started to learn about the culture from the Internet, Indian people that we met, staff at Indian restaurants. India became a part of our lives even before we had been allocated a child.

When our file was almost ready to be sent to India we had a phone call from the adoption agency. They had three siblings available and would we consider adopting them?

We had stated we would accept siblings, expecting two not three children. At the time these children were nearly two, four and six years. There were two boys and a little girl. I had always wanted a little girl. In some ways to have three children would be a dream come true. But going from no children to three would be a big challenge. The other issue for me was the age of the eldest child. At 25 I didn't feel ready to parent a six-year-old boy.

We vacillated, discussing the positives and negatives. Finally we decided not to accept the offer. We weren't ready for three children at once. From time to time we wondered what would have happened if we had accepted but felt no regrets about the decision we made. We never found out what happened to the children. We like to think that they were adopted into a loving caring family somewhere in Australia.

Our file left for India. The wait for allocation wasn't too difficult. We were busy at work and I enjoyed my job. At times we wondered how much longer it would be but most of the time we were fairly relaxed.

Our file had been in India for about four or five months when the adoption agency rang with our allocation. Words can't explain the feelings in response to the call. I was so excited I was shaking. It was a little girl, which was very exciting for me. As my husband and I worked together I went to tell him the news. Then we drove straight to the adoption agency to find out about her. She was born in September 1996 and would be a little over four by the time we would collect her. Her name was Ganga Bhavani. We liked her names and decided to swap her first and middle names around. We had a couple of photos of her and she looked absolutely gorgeous. We eagerly signed the paperwork and headed straight to my parents' house. They were as excited as we were. Back at work we told everyone. For us it was like announcing a pregnancy, as no one there knew of our plans to adopt. Everyone shared our happiness.

We busied ourselves with the preparations of bringing our little girl home. There were flights to arrange, and accommodation and travel within India. We had planned to see the Taj Mahal. When we arrived back Bhavani would be old enough to start kindergarten, so we enrolled her. I bought toys and clothes. I couldn't wait to have her with me so we could go shopping together. Our lives seemed to centre on bringing Bhavani home.

We were due to collect our little girl from India in January 2001. But in November we had a call from the adoption agency with news that turned our world around. Our little girl had tested positive for HIV. I was at home by myself when I received the call. I couldn't think what to do. My husband and I were devastated. We arranged for the day off and went to the adoption agency where we were told there was no doubt that Bhavani was HIV positive. We had no decision to make. Bhavani would not be granted entry into Australia. We couldn't adopt this little girl who we already thought of as our daughter. The staff at the adoption agency were supportive; they were also upset by the news. On the way home we stopped at my parents' house to let them know.

We didn't know what to do. We were overcome with grief for our own loss but also thought of the poor little girl in India who had seen our photos, thought she would have a mummy and daddy and a new life, and then for no reason that she could understand had lost it all. And she would get sick and we would be helpless to do anything to help her. The adoption agency told us that the orphanage where Bhavani lived was trying to find her biological parents to place her back in their care. More awful news, as they would not have had the money to care for a sick child. We enquired about offering financial assistance for Bhavani but there were no guarantees that the money would reach her, so we decided against this idea. Months later, adoption from this orphanage ceased. We never found out what happened to Bhavani. We can only wonder and feel a little sad each time.

The hardest thing for me was the constant reminder. I had told many of the people I worked with that we were adopting a little girl from India. People would come in and ask how things were going. Repeating the story was emotionally draining. Some days were difficult just going to the shopping centre and seeing all those mums with their children, something that I had dreamed of.

A few days after we received the bad news my husband and I asked to have our file taken out of India. On one hand we wanted another allocation immediately and on the other, we wanted our little girl back. We just weren't emotionally ready to continue with the adoption process. It felt like we had hit a brick wall.

Over the next month we discussed what to do. We knew that if we wanted a child we would have to get back into the adoption process, no matter how emotionally difficult it might be. We were no longer relaxed about time frames. I had turned 26. It seemed ironic that we had worried about my not being old enough to adopt at the beginning of the process. Then we had assumed that we would have a child by the time I was 25 but no later than 26.

We went back to the agency to talk about our options. The age regulations were due to be changed at the end of January so this opened up other countries for us. There could now be up to 45 years between the child's and my husband's age, meaning we could adopt a much younger child. It also meant we could choose Korea.

The first thing I did was buy the Lonely Planet to Seoul. I wanted to know what our future child might look like. Our file left for Korea in February 2001. I kept in regular contact with the adoption agency, and one day after I rang, I ran out to tell my husband I had a gut feeling the agency had news it couldn't tell me – but I thought it was a girl. The next week we had a call from the agency and yes, it was a girl! We were both over the moon. Later the agency told us they had found out the day I telephoned and the person I spoke to wasn't officially able to inform us. She had found it hard keeping the good news from us.

The agency showed us her photograph and we could see that

she was a very happy and healthy baby. Her name was Kim Hee Jin, which means truth and hope.

The process after allocation from Korea was different. We tried unsuccessfully not to get emotionally attached, in fear that something might go wrong. We prepared as much as we could for our new arrival. We both had a lot to learn; neither of us knew anything about caring for babies. We had prepared ourselves for the challenges of parenting a four-year-old, not a four-month-old. I bought only the bare necessities. However as the time approached we became more and more excited. We chose a name for our little girl, however we agreed that we would wait to meet her to see if her name suited. In the meantime we called her Hee Jin.

Finally the time came to travel to Korea to bring Hee Jin home. We arrived in Korea on the Saturday but weren't due to meet her until the Monday. On the Sunday we found our way to the Korean adoption agency so we would be prepared for the following day. We fell in love with the Korean people straight away. We found them to be extremely helpful and very passionate people.

On the Monday we were up early and heading for the subway station to meet Hee Jin. We were excited and nervous. We arrived about ten minutes early and while we were waiting I recognised the foster mother of our little girl. And then there she was in the foster mother's arms! We went to one of the meeting rooms so we could all be together. Hee Jin had changed a lot from the photo we had first seen only about three months earlier. She was a placid baby and came to us easily. In line with the process, we left our little girl in the care of her foster family while we spent our last holiday together as a couple. We took in as much as we could of Korea and have many treasured memories to share with Hee Jin as she grows up.

The day came for us all to go home together as a family. As we drove to the airport with our little girl on my lap I was overcome with emotion. I knew for sure that we had finally made it. Except that it was just the beginning . . .

When I look back at the process of adoption I am amazed at all the emotions we experienced and sometimes wonder how we made it through. I believe that we were meant to have this little girl and she was meant to have us. The road might have been a bit curvy but we crossed paths in the end. Was it worth it? All I have to do is look at my little girl and yes, definitely, I would do it all again. The joy that she has brought us has made us who we are today.

PS: Since writing our story we began the process all over again and were allocated a little boy, this time from Thailand. We were meant to travel to Thailand in May of 2005 but actually went in March. The process wasn't as challenging as the first time but also not a smooth ride. Life has been quite hectic, not that I'm complaining. We are all settling. My daughter broke her toe a week after we arrived home from Thailand, just to add to the excitement!

Leaps of faith

Bessie Smith

When you marry late in life, as we did, the reality that children may not be part of your life together becomes glaringly obvious. Our infertility impacted mostly on me because my partner had a biological child from his first marriage. His grief was more about the belief that he had let me down. I grieved alone, finding that most people found the subject uncomfortable. I would wander around baby departments in stores touching all the baby clothes.

Our life as a married couple was socially full and awash with consumerism. It was on an overseas trip, languishing by a pool, that my partner read an article in a local paper.

'Thirty babies a day abandoned at local orphanage,' he said. 'You know we should go and look, it can't be far from here.'

We made the visit the next day. I remember it was very hot, and we were astounded at how many children there were, about a hundred, with their beautiful dark eyes. They chattered; many grabbed and pulled at us. One little boy put his hand in mine. We just wanted to pick them all up and take them home. In the nursery there were about 30 babies sleeping in cots. The staff said they were short of basic necessities like nappies. The room was very stark; no beautiful linen, no nursery murals on the walls, no chests stuffed with toys and books, just row after row of babies in basic white metal cots.

We could not stay long in there, it was too confronting; so many orphaned babies, it seemed so cruel and illogical. We both became quite emotional. But we came away thoughtful about the idea of adopting a baby.

Once back home we did at times question our decision, particularly after our first interview with the adoption agency when we realised the process was going to be more arduous than we had at first imagined. We could not adopt from our chosen country, nor choose the sex of the child.

We felt that our options were once again being narrowed. At one point we even pulled out because of a family illness, but the grief was just unbearable. It was like being told all over again that we couldn't have children, like a door slamming in our face! So we contacted the adoption agency again and asked for our file to be reinstated. We hadn't realised the extent to which we had again started to hope that we would have a child.

My partner had spent many years in Asia, had encountered poverty. He never questioned adopting an Asian child. But for me, after the initial euphoria waned, I had to really ponder whether I could love another woman's child as my own.

Eventually I figured that I wasn't particularly concerned about reproducing our own gene pool, as that had been done plentifully by my sisters. I felt that part of my infertility was subconsciously fuelled by the guilt of bringing a child into such a troubled world. By adopting, I rationalised that I could help a child already born, and some semblance of balance might be restored. Once we had made this leap of faith it was remarkable how easily those lovely dreamy conversations we had lying nestled in bed as a childless couple, changed from 'pregnancy dreams' to wonderment about what our adopted child would be like.

It took nearly two years but we eventually travelled overseas to bring home a little boy. He'd had a rocky past, but it was testament to what a forgiving, loving little soul he is, and terribly humbling, how at our first meeting he came to us with a shy but genuinely warm and trusting manner. My partner and I were overcome with emotion as this little boy readily slipped his hand into ours and we led him away from all he had known.

Our son is a bright boy with a wonderful, caring, gentle nature and a great sense of fun. He has given us back triple-fold anything we had hoped to give him. And now, looking at my beautiful boy lying blissfully asleep in bed, I bend down and put my face in the nape of his neck and inhale the smell of him, and realise what a remarkable journey we have made. How the pain of infertility has faded, replaced by the brilliance of our little boy. Our son.

PS from our son: The story was okay and being adopted is okay. The best thing about being adopted is getting a new family, but the mangoes taste better back home.

Seoul searching

Lisa Saxby

Like most couples, we thought we could control the start of our family. We waited until we had completed tertiary studies, travelled overseas, made a dent in our mortgage and completed house renovations before we decided the time was right. After a year of trying we became concerned that we hadn't achieved a pregnancy. Then, after the usual tests failed to provide an explanation, our doctor referred us to a specialist, who performed further tests, also inconclusive, and an operation on me to check my Fallopian tubes, which were fine. By this time, I was starting to feel anxious, upset and depressed. What seemed so easy for most people was looking impossible for us.

We had begun to consider other options. I had requested information about intercountry adoption and we'd made an appointment with a reproductive medicine clinic when, much to our delight, we got pregnant all by ourselves! We were so excited we could barely contain ourselves. Even though we knew it was still early days, we began to talk about names and when I'd start maternity leave. After only a couple of weeks we decided to share our wonderful secret with our immediate family because my husband's parents had both been ill. We thought our news would give them a boost. Needless to say, they were thrilled.

When I had my first scan I was reassured to see the little dot's steady pulsing heartbeat. We were given a printout and told our baby's due date. I felt more confident and relaxed. I went along to my next appointment feeling well and looking forward to having another scan to see the baby again. However, this time our little dot wasn't pulsing.

'This isn't what you want to hear but I'm afraid your baby has died,' the doctor said. We were shocked and devastated. It was hard to take it in. I had to have surgery the next day. This was the worst thing that had ever happened to us. I felt like a failure and wondered if it was my fault. Tests provided no answers. I returned to work just days after, crying in the car all the way there, barely keeping it together during the day, then crying all the way home again. They were dark days and I sometimes wondered if I'd ever get through them.

It was particularly cruel that around this time there seemed to be a population explosion amongst friends, family and acquaintances. One baby was even due on the same day as ours. I felt like we were being punished, but I couldn't think what for. Three months later we started trying again: temperature charts, herbal preparations, rose quartz crystals, eliminating certain foods from our diet, adding others, and vitamins as well. I always thought I was a bit of a sceptic, but I would give anything I thought might be a fertility idol a rub for good luck!

It still wasn't happening and we decided to be more proactive and try to have more control over our situation. We made another appointment with the reproductive medicine clinic and an appointment to speak to someone at the adoption agency. I will never forget how excited and encouraged we felt after that first information session. There were several real, live families at the agency that evening and meeting them was uplifting. We soon realised that providing we met all the criteria, it was more a case of when it would happen, rather than if. We felt quite sure that intercountry adoption was for us. Our appointments at the clinic had left us feeling flat and without confidence. When we told the doctor that we had decided not to go ahead with IVF, that we wanted to adopt instead, he said he thought we might regret not trying at least one cycle of IVF and warned us of the expense of intercountry adoption. We politely explained that our decision was well considered and we were aware of the costs involved.

Once we had chosen our path, we couldn't get through the process quickly enough. We were so keen, we would complete and return any paperwork as soon as possible, often by return mail. Going through the process was exciting and anxiety provoking, even though ours was a comparatively short wait of 15 months. We had chosen to send our file to Korea after discussing our options with the agency here. While waiting, we began to embrace our child's birth culture. We spoke to other couples who had adopted and read over 20 books on the subject.

Many of the books contained contributions from adopted individuals, birth parents and adoptive parents. Most of the case studies seemed to focus on the negative aspects of intercountry adoption – this concerned me, and made me think hard about what we were doing. It seemed there was often resentment from the child toward the adoptive parents. I wondered if it was a selfish thing we were planning.

I remember vividly how ecstatic we were at allocation. I held my breath for a moment when the agency rang that morning because I thought there might be a problem. Instead they told me we had a son. My mind raced as I scribbled every bit of information about him in the margin of the TV guide. I called my husband at work to tell him the good news, blurting it out at 100 miles an hour! His colleagues congratulated him. I collected him and we made our way into town. It was Harmony Day, a day to celebrate diversity and racial harmony.

It was so exciting to see our son's photo for the first time and to read about his routine, health, weight, height, even his bowel movements. Later that day we dropped in to share our news with family members. It was like telling them they'd won lotto! We had about 30 copies made of our son's photo and put it on either side of our bed, on the fridge, in my husband's wallet and in my purse. At last it was actually going to happen, we could finally go out and buy all the baby paraphernalia that we'd been too super-stitious to even look at. Our families threw us a baby shower on our son's one hundredth day. This is a significant day in Korean culture and is usually a celebrated milestone. We were desperate to find out how soon we could travel.

When we did get the go ahead to travel to Korea, the trip was a bit surreal. It's a wonderful place with polite and welcoming people. However, I was concerned that we weren't off to the best start as a family. We had only one brief visit with our son, at his foster parent's house, then we didn't see him again for five days when, after a hurried blessing and hand-over, we were whisked away to the airport. It felt wrong to be ripping him away from all that was familiar. I wondered if the transition would have been easier if we had been allowed more contact with him during our stay and if the hand-over had been the day before we had to travel home. It left me feeling rather shell-shocked. I was sad for his foster mother and worried that he would reject us but at the same time, elated to finally have him in our arms.

Although he was only four-and-a-half months old, our son had a very strong attachment to his foster family and by the time we reached Singapore, he had become extremely distressed. I sought reassurance from the medical centre at Changi Airport to eliminate any physical cause for his upset. In the early days at home we had quite a few episodes like this; he seemed inconsolable at times. Many people had said he would adjust to us easily because he was young, but I believe it took time. Fortunately he did begin to trust us and words can't adequately describe how good it felt when he started to accept comfort from us or put his arms out for us to hold him.

I remember when we'd been home just over a week and went to a gathering of friends. It was one of the first occasions he clearly expressed his preference for me over all of the other people in the room. His eyes followed me as he was taken and introduced to everyone and he soon became upset if he couldn't see me for even a few seconds. When he was back in my arms he seemed to relax and become more settled. This was a break-through. I wasn't just another blurry stranger's face in the crowd. I was his mum.

We believe the three of us are meant to be together and we feel truly blessed to have such a beautiful, wondrous, lovable child in our lives. He still gets upset sometimes and there are occasions when I wonder if it's simply due to frustration, his stage of development, pain or illness, or if maybe he still has some pent-up emotions regarding his early days.

I'm sure we've many more challenges to face as a family, however I would add that any difficult times are compensated 10,000 fold just by having him in our lives. When well-meaning strangers tell us what a lucky boy he is, we always correct them: 'We're the lucky ones.'

PS: Since this story was written our new daughter from China has joined the family.

Running until she finishes

Belinda Shaw

On a warm tropical morning I was folding the washing when the phone rang. It was the adoption agency. We had just completed 12 months of paperwork, assessments and seminars and I assumed they merely wanted more information. Instead it was the phone call that changed our lives.

'How would you like a little girl?' I thought they were kidding! Then I just collapsed and cried. We had been told that an allocation from India would take six to 12 months. We had only been waiting six weeks! I said yes and rang Tim. His reaction was the same as mine. After a few tears over the phone we hung up and were quite numb for the rest of the day.

We were told that it would still be four to five months before we could travel to India to bring home our daughter. That was hard as she was only four months old at allocation and we wanted her with us as soon as possible. But with the Indian procedures and court process there wasn't much we could do but wait.

A couple of months into that waiting time we received a letter from the adoption agency. It was devastating news. Adoptions in India had been banned until further notice due to investigations, and our orphanage was involved.

The orphanage was investigated and found reputable and the ban was lifted three months later. However, our daughter's file had not progressed and so it meant another agonising wait. Weeks went by without any news. This was the toughest time.

When we did receive bits of news we went through every emotion from total despair to jubilation. You think you will cope with whatever happens but there are days when you wonder what on earth you have done.

We were fortunate to receive videos of our daughter during this time. It didn't help our emotions, but it was at least reassuring to have these updates. The court procedures were taking an eternity. Finally we had a departure date and had started to buy baby clothes and equipment. We were off to bring our baby home.

Two weeks before we left for India the adoption agency phoned. I was wondering what else could go wrong, but this time we were asked if we could be in India by the end of the week! We spent the next few days frantically re-organising our arrangements. Our travel agent was absolutely wonderful. I collected the tickets on the morning we flew out.

Arriving in India in the early hours of the morning was an experience. The airport was crowded. When we came through the gates we were relieved to see our name held up on a piece of paper above the sea of faces. We were taken to our hotel, settled in and told that we would be meeting our daughter at nine o'clock the next morning. There was a woman staying at the same hotel who had been in India for about a month and had collected her daughter a week earlier. This was great as she would be able to 'show us the ropes'. It turned out we would be returning home all together.

The next morning we were nervous and tired from the emotional week and long journey. As instructed, we stayed in our room to wait for our daughter to arrive. The morning passed and we continued to wait. Then the woman from next door came and told us the orphanage had contacted her and informed her that there had been a bomb on the train and our daughter was coming later in the afternoon. It wasn't long, though, before we heard a knock. We answered it to two men holding our beautiful daughter. I just cried and she took one look at me and began to cry too. I tried not to rush her. We sat on the bed together and I put out my arms to her and she came to me. I fed her and she relaxed and we had a wonderful first cuddle.

After about ten minutes the two men left us, and our daughter screamed. I managed to calm her and she clung to me. It was very special. We bathed her as she was quite dirty and had lice in her hair. She hated the bath and screamed at that too. We persisted and then gave her another bottle. By this stage she was relaxing with us a little more. Well, with me anyway. Every time Tim spoke or looked at her she screamed at him. I couldn't leave the room without her screaming. Fortunately this only lasted a couple of days and she calmed down. It was awful for a while but we got through it.

We were told that it was safer to stay in our room as tourists were uncommon in this region. We did not mind this as it gave us a chance to get to know our daughter and for her to know us. With the help of our driver we did manage to do some sightseeing and (of course!) shopping.

Later in the week we travelled to New Delhi to collect a travel visa from the Australian embassy. We also saw the Taj Mahal and did more shopping. We were apprehensive at the thought of going to India as it was well outside our comfort zone. But once there we found it a fascinating place and we really enjoyed it – and we brought home the best present ever!

Once home our daughter settled well. She slept 12 hours each night and was happy. She was not crawling or sitting up when we collected her and, at 13 months old, this was a problem. Investigations revealed mild cerebral palsy affecting both her legs and her right side. Fortunately, this did not scare us. We had experience with this condition and knew that the path ahead was therapy and more therapy.

We have faced many challenges with our daughter, like teaching her to do the things most children do naturally: crawling, walking and riding a bike. We are constantly reminding her to use both hands and we incorporate her therapy into our daily routine. Through all the challenges we have experienced many joys. The one joy that will remain in my mind forever is the day she ran a race at school. I wasn't sure about it but the teacher said she really wanted to do it. She came last but didn't give up and just ran until she finished. I waited at the finish line and heard the whole school cheering her on. She just fell into my arms and I burst into tears and could not stop crying. I was so proud of her. The look on her face when she achieved her goal made all the difficult times worthwhile.

Our daughter is now six and showing amazing progress. She is a very determined and stubborn little girl but we feel this is an advantage for her. She takes everything in her stride and makes us extremely proud.

We have told her of her adoption and that she has a birth mother in India. Our aim one day is to take her back to India and hopefully to meet with her birth mother. We will always be honest with our daughter and look forward to continuing our journey. It never ends really, it just changes course.

After some unsuccessful attempts on IVF over the next few years we decided to adopt again. Although we had a difficult time with our daughter we were excited at the prospect of having another baby in the house. We began the paperwork for India again, only this time it would be a different orphanage. Our file went and once again the waiting began.

After a couple of months we were told that we had been matched with a baby boy. This was great news, though we couldn't believe it was all happening so fast. However we were told the allocation would take some time, as the baby was very young. India also has regulations regarding the relinquishing mother and this was affecting our case. As time went by the allocation time was repeatedly postponed. It was all coming back to us; could we handle it a second time?

Then there was the issue of the health of the children coming out of India. We already had a child with special needs, was it fair knowingly to take on another child who may have special needs? We had not seen a photo as we had not yet been formally allocated, so we could not find out if the baby boy was healthy. We could not take the risk. So after many discussions with family, friends and professionals we made the decision to change country. We felt the pain of not accepting this boy but we knew he would be allocated to another family. I understand he was and all is well.

We completed all the paperwork for Korea, our only other choice. Our file was sent and once again the waiting began. The

Korean program was more efficient and enjoyable, though not without its challenges.

My most memorable image of our time in Korea is when we were taken to the foster mother's home to meet our son. As we were driving around the small streets of Seoul we passed some people on the side of the road. In an instant we knew which one was our boy. Out of all those people we knew our son! Later in the foster mother's house our gorgeous son was placed in my arms and he fell asleep.

We began this parenting journey not knowing if we would ever have children. Now we have been blessed with two beautiful children and a wonderful story to share.

PS from our daughter, now seven years old, who wanted to add that she loved it when her parents came to get her from India.

Conflict

Perhaps it was wrong of us to remove her from the only security she had, just to satisfy our own desires to have a child.

Mee and me: adapting to adoptive motherhood

Pam Sharpe

There she is! We are studying a photograph of a small Korean girl in a pale yellow dress with a winning smile. Nine-and-a-half months old with a twinkle in her eye that is older than her years. This is the first time we have seen our daughter-to-be.

Yet I'm not easily won over. We have been trying to have a biological child for years. By now I'm physically and psychologically worn down by investigations, operations and IVF procedures spanning two continents. Much of this has been a torment I haven't wanted to share, although latterly we joined a support group where we talked around the medical processes and tried to will ourselves out of a sort of communal misery. Some of the people who attended the group would never settle for anything but their own biological children – but as medical assessment of our case has become more and more pessimistic, we have decided that adoption is the only way that we will ever have children.

The overseas adoption process is no joke. We soon come up against the law that says there can be no more than a 40-year gap between child and oldest parent. As almost everyone knows, adoption requires a vast amount of repetitious paperwork and bureaucracy. While we are wading through that, we are simultaneously lobbying the state parliament to change the law that might make it impossible for us to adopt a baby. And then there is the assessment process. For two or three harrowing hours every week, for what seems to be an endless number of weeks, a psychologist questions us. We come to dread these hours because every area of our life – sex life, finances, and our childhood – is discussed and assessed. Finally the results are condensed into a long report and sent to a committee who will decide whether or not we are fit people to adopt. Most couples (or single people) do not 'pass' first time and have to answer questions or prepare more material for another meeting.

While all this has been happening, I have plenty of time to reflect on a fundamental question. Do I want children? We have deliberately chosen to start a family late because we did not find any gap in our lives. Indeed life seemed full and interesting and rewarding without children. We love to travel. We both have professional jobs and ambitions and often they leave little spare time. I've always avoided too much conversation with those who can only talk about babies and children. We have had some wonderful opportunities such as consulting on an aid project, which meant we lived in a missionary hospital in a remote part of rural Tanzania for a few fascinating months. Both malaria and AIDS struck the area and I doubt that we would ever have gone there with young children.

So what am I doing? Perhaps all the years of infertility treatment and then the tortures of the adoption process just added up to a perverse desire not to be beaten by something. Also my husband wants children. So now we are on a plane to Seoul to pick up the girl in the yellow dress with the winning smile. Things have gone into fast-forward since we saw that photograph. The South Korean–Australian adoption program, going strong for over 30 years, caters for under-ones and our daughter (as we will come to know her) will be eleven-and-a-half months by the time we meet her. Normally children from this particular orphanage are allocated at about eight weeks. This would have happened to Mee-Yeon, but something went wrong with her previous allocation.

Now we are told to report to a certain room in the orphanage to meet our daughter. We see her before we enter the room. She is a little round person on the knee of her foster mother dressed in a 'Reds' outfit from the recent World Cup soccer in Seoul. Her hair is in an upstanding ponytail and she is eating a packet of crisps. We are supposed to fall in love with her now ... but, as yet, we don't.

A social worker translates what the foster mother, Mrs Choo, can tell us about this girl. She is thought to be an 'easy baby'. But this is a supermother talking. Fifty-four years old, she has raised two of her own children and fostered 60. This tough-looking lady must know all there is to know about the ways of babies. I have only read Penelope Leach because I did not want to sound wholly ignorant when quizzed by the dreaded psychologist. Like revision for my school exams, I now remember nothing of what I read.

We are taken on a tour of the orphanage. I'm allowed to carry Mee-Yeon. There is no bonding. Mee-Yeon is content enough to be carried, but relieved to be returned to her foster mother who carries her in the traditional Korean way, on a sling on her back. Having been carried this way for almost a year, Mee-Yeon expertly hoists herself onto Mrs Choo's back and they head home through the urban maze.

We take the customary idea of seeing the country seriously. We sightsee energetically (and try many varieties of local food) and then we board a train and head south to stay in a Korean guest-house and bicycle around an historic area. I am in my element with this part of the adoptive parenting process. I'm only too keen to absorb all aspects of Korean history and culture so that I can tell Mee-Yeon about them when she is old enough to want to know.

But in the back of my mind are nagging doubts. Almost all the seminars we attended as part of the adoption process have concentrated on the negative aspects of the process. We have watched a horrifying video about children adopted from the hellhole orphanages of Ceauçescu's Romania. We have talked with a woman with two 'problem' Russian children for whom life will never again approach normal. We have had a seminar from an older adopted man who, when he started to investigate his background, opened a can of worms with implications across continents. I have read Nancy Verrier's book *The Primal Wound* where she claims that adopted children never recover from some sort of enduring attachment to the mother who carries them for nine months and then gives birth to them. I am convinced that Verrier is stressing nature over nurture but as a woman who has never given birth, how can I really say? We certainly don't come across too many biological mothers talking about how they haven't bonded with their bundle of joy, do we?

At every stage of the process, we have been forced to think, read, attend courses and talk about something that is summed up in the word 'attachment'. I have so much information on the difficulties adopted children face bonding with their adoptive parents (and in many cases there may be physiological reasons for this) that I have no idea how Mee-Yeon can possibly attach to us. And the primary question for me seems to be, can I attach to her?

When we return from the holiday in the south we are invited to see Mee-Yeon again at her foster mother's house. A feast of traditional Korean food is laid out for us. Mee-Yeon is told that we are mummy and daddy but she is reluctant to engage with us at all, although she is very interested in the food. She has already assumed a demeanour of inscrutability that (with hindsight) was to characterise her for her first three months with us.

This is just two days before departure. A couple of rushed days of activity follow. I wanted to see Mee-Yeons's birthplace and the agency where she was taken in. I knew that it would be important to talk about these things to my daughter later on.

On the day of departure, we gather in the foyer of the orphanage for a prayer with the Methodist founder of the institution and the foster mother. Although she has done this 59 times before and appears to be of stoic character, Mrs Choo is very upset indeed. Tears are streaming down her face as we get into the bus to take us to the airport. Our girl is placed in my arms and promptly falls asleep.

We expected the journey to be hell. Mee-Yeon is old enough to know that something dramatic has just happened. How on earth will we comfort a little person in such profound distress? At the airport she starts to scream when she realises that we are not conversing with her in Korean but once the plane is in motion, she settles into a deep slumber in my arms. This is perhaps the first hint we have that the orphanage lady who matches children with parents in the orphanage knows what she is doing. We have a girl who positively relaxes when travelling long distances.

Mrs Choo has added a large bag to the kit of essential nappies, formula and so on that the orphanage supplies for the trip. The bag is full of Mee-Yeon's favourite chocolate cake. Over the first few days at home, we have many tea parties as friends visit to see Mee-Yeon and the chocolate cake is a clear winner as far as bonding is concerned. I wonder why, during all the serious hours of pondering about psychological approaches to 'attachment', chocolate cake was never mentioned.

We have only been home a week when we are invited to the Korean community's preparations for Harvest Moon where rice cakes will be made. We are overwhelmed by the enthusiasm with which Mee-Yeon is greeted but the interesting thing is that although everyone but us looks Korean and speaks Korean, Mee-Yeon already knows that we are her parents and keeps coming to us. And only two weeks after she arrives we celebrate Mee-Yeon's first birthday in the best traditional Korean style that we can manage (because to Koreans it is the first and sixtieth birthdays that really count). Mee-Yeon is dressed in her *hanbok*, her Korean traditional dress, given to us by Mrs Choo. She assumes an air of formality but again there is no doubt that for the purposes of recognition, she has attached to us.

It was still the case that coming to love Mee-Yeon was a slow, accumulating process for us. Derek had to return to work only a few days after we came back from Seoul. I was on maternity leave, yet instead of a tiny helpless baby, I had a rumbustious toddler to contend with. She was heavy to carry and I soon had a strained wrist from this effort. Mee-Yeon is no dainty Asian girl. One evening after a day of hell, when it later transpired that Mee-Yeon was cutting a tooth, I stormed off to the beach in a state of despair. Shortly after this, Mee-Yeon contracted chicken-pox and spent whole days screaming with her mother screaming inwardly at the same time.

I have never, and will never, enjoy childcare. I had a spell of part-time work but gleefully returned to full-time when Mee-Yeon settled down at a nursery. It is now two years since we returned from Seoul. During this time, we have had the opportunity to travel extensively with Mee-Yeon. In fact, she had been to all five continents by the time she was two. She also had a life-threatening illness. For a week time was suspended as she battled pneumonia in the intensive care ward of the Children's Hospital. I still really don't know whether or not I have a maternal instinct. But as the months went past, Mee-Yeon's inscrutability lifted and a little character started to emerge, a friendly, funny girl with engaging eyes and a lovely smile who could say *happy* and *cuddle* and *special mummy and daddy*.

And something started to happen to me. My upbringing, the years of travel and career development and, perhaps most of all, becoming inured to the endless cycle of failure that is implicit in infertility gave me a sort of emotional armoury that was hard to shake off. I've not entirely lost that – it has some advantages – but I've certainly become more emotionally attuned. There is no turning point here, just a slow accretion of likable love.

I'm the third mother to come along for Mee-Yeon. First there was the woman who carried her for nine months. Unmarried motherhood is still stigmatised in South Korea. We will probably never know much about that pregnancy but we are aware that her mother must have made a clear choice not to have an abortion, carried Mee-Yeon until birth, made advance arrangements with a very good orphanage, and even made a choice of the overseas country that she wished her daughter to go to. Then there was Mrs Choo, that tough and practical supermother extraordinaire. And finally the bundle of insecurity that was me. The last 18 months have not been easy but I can honestly say that the times of panic and despair have been pierced by moments of intense joy and love. I've become a committed advocate and activist for adoption. I have a much broader and deeper understanding of many issues, from child health to Korean culture. Perhaps above all, those of us who adopt are really in a position to confront and challenge some modern ideologies of motherhood head on.

Mee-Yeon was our first child. But one enormous surprise is that I am expecting a sibling for her in the near future as a result of a natural pregnancy. The road so far has been a rugged one but it has certainly been a life-changing experience for Mee and me.

At this stage I'm assured of the sincerity of my little girl's winning smile and I smile back readily. And behind those smiles, there is an enormous reservoir of love on both sides.

PS: After this story was written our second daughter, Freya, was born and, so far, Mee-Yeon loves having a little sister around.

The other mothers

Deb McDowall

The call came on 19 September 2000. It was a Tuesday. I was working in my office, preparing for the orientation program I was facilitating the next day. I answered the telephone with my usual spiel. The voice on the other end replied, 'Hello Deb. It's Rachel from the agency.' My heart stood still, I took a huge breath and tried to breathe again, but nothing happened. The voice continued, 'Can you talk?'

'Yes,' I replied tentatively, trying to control the tiny little breaths stacking one on the other as they ascended into a sigh. Tears streamed down my face in anticipation of what may follow.

'Deb, you have a son!'

We arrived in Seoul, South Korea, three months later to meet the tiny little person who had consumed my every thought since Rachel's call, to hold him, to love him, to bring him home to Adelaide and to begin our journey as a family of three.

The morning of our first meeting I was so excited. Not scared. Not overwhelmed. Just ready. There were several foster mothers in the open-plan offices on Level 2, each with a tiny bundle snuggled on their back, chatting to social workers and other office staff. I surveyed the room, hoping to catch a glimpse of Hyeon-Cheol. And then I did. He was so beautiful to me. I remember the goose bumps running up my arms, making me shiver as they reached my body. Mrs Jeong, our social worker, came to meet us and directed us towards a small meeting room, where Mrs Lee and Hyeon-Cheol were waiting. Mrs Lee smiled so warmly at us, her eyes full of love as she looked at Hyeon-Cheol and chatted to him softly.

'*Uhm-ma. Ap-ba,*' she repeated to him, as she motioned towards us. Mrs Lee had loved, nurtured, and cared for this little baby she cradled so fondly in her arms since he was two weeks old. To hear her refer to me as 'Mummy' triggered the realisation that within the next week, we would be taking him from her. As this thought sobered my elation, Mrs Lee bounced Hyeon-Cheol from her lap to my own. My elation resurfaced, and thoughts of the impact of our son's adoption were swept aside, temporarily. I gazed at his tiny face, touched his little fingers, and held him tightly. 'Soon you will be my son,' I thought, 'my beautiful baby boy, for ever and ever.'

Later the same day, as I was fossicking though the bookcase in the guest house, I came across an anthology of letters entitled *I Wish For You a Beautiful Life* written by Korean women to children they had relinquished for adoption. I started to read it, and couldn't put it down. Each letter drew me in closer to their hearts, to their pain, and revealed the cultural and social forces contributing to their decision to relinquish their child. My earlier thoughts were based on my perception of the 'Korean way', not on insights into a mother's heart. It was like an awakening for me. A realisation that the tiny baby I was about to call my own was a son to three mothers, each with different opportunities to express their love for him.

On Christmas Eve 2000, Mrs Lee held Hyeon-Cheol in her arms for the last time. Her lips pressed gently and repeatedly over his face, like a butterfly dancing on the delicate petals of a flower, and then she handed him to me. I had no words to say to her, I could not speak. I only hope my expression conveyed the depth of my love for him, my gratitude to her for loving him so dearly, and my promise to always keep him safe.

That night, as we tried unsuccessfully to get some sleep, I gazed endlessly at the tiny little angel snuggled in bed between us, and pondered how his other mothers were feeling; one who was without him for the first time in four-and-a-half months, and the other who had held him in her heart since the time of his conception, but only briefly in her arms.

Once home in Adelaide, we began to discover the joys and challenges of parenting. It was wonderful, every sleepless moment of it! I quickly got into the swing of bottles, nappies, baby baths, lullabies, settling, resettling, and settling again, and soon felt comfortable with the 'doings' of being a mum. The 'feelings' of being a mum were, however, quite a different story. I felt overwhelmed by the depth of my love towards our son. It was as though he was the only thing I was living for and, although I adore my husband, there appeared in my mind no comparison between the two. Lachlan Hyeon-Cheol was my whole world. It took many, many months for me to come to terms with the depth of my feelings for him. It wasn't that I hadn't anticipated loving him. I, like many adoptive parents (and indeed my husband), had fallen in love with his allocation photo and, too, with the notion that we would soon be parents. It was the purity of my love for him that took me by complete surprise, the unconditional love of a parent for their child.

I delighted in the minutiae of motherhood, but the thought of Hyeon-Cheol's other mothers never left me. The notion plagued me that his birth mother was somewhere in South Korea, endeavouring to go about her business as though she had not endured the heartache of separation from a much-loved child, all the while crying in pain on the inside for a child who may never feel the depth of her love. I recalled the words of one birth mother from the book I had read: *I can endure anything if it is for your happiness, my dear. I can endure anything if it is for your good future. As my mother used to say, this is the way for you ...*

These words tumbled over and over in my head. Happy, happy! Must keep him happy to ensure she who gave life to him, can endure her own without him.

Several weeks after our return home we were invited to speak regarding our experience with the Korean program and as new parents at the adoption agency's orientation program for prospective adoptive parents. All was proceeding well until I began to venture down the unspoken track. 'I think about Lachlan Hyeon-Cheol's birth mother all the time ...' Unfortunately, as is the way with me, I started to cry and could no longer speak. I looked at John for assistance, hoping he would save me, but he just squeezed my hand tightly and smiled back. Warm and loving but hardly a knight in shining armour! Those moments of silence seemed to last forever, until the program's facilitator spoke. I regret this issue was not explored further, that I had not done all I wanted to plant the notion of the seemingly forgotten parties, the 'other mothers', in the minds of those embarking on their adoption journey.

My concern for Lachlan Hyeon-Cheol's birth mother simmered over the months ahead, and then exploded as we endeavoured to celebrate Lachlan's first birthday. It was a day of great joy and deep, deep sorrow for me. I cried for most of the morning, connecting with her pain, trying to tell her (telepathically, I guess) that he was well, that he was happy, and that he was dearly, oh so dearly loved. She was so inexplicably entwined in my mind, in my life. I wondered whether she felt the same of me.

I thought, too, of Mrs Lee, Lachlan Hyeon-Cheol's foster mother. I later learned that in all probability she would have been given another baby to foster just days after we left with Hyeon-Cheol, and that this cycle would keep repeating until she was unable to continue her work as a foster mother. Although I took comfort in this knowledge, I knew she would still have a special place in her heart for all the children she had previously fostered, including Hyeon-Cheol. I wrote her a lengthy letter about Lachlan's progress and our feelings for him and, indeed, for her, and sent a small album of photos, which I continue to do every year around Christmas. I decided to also send a brief overview and a collection of photos to the Korean agency at the same time for inclusion in Hyeon-Cheol's file just in case his birth mother had the opportunity to check his progress.

In February 2004 I returned to Seoul, this time with my mother, to be united with our second son, Min Yeong. I had been warned by several mothers, each of them mothers of biological children, that one's feelings for the second child may not be quite the same as for the first. Certainly, I was not as overwhelmed by my feelings for Min Yeong, but they were just as deep, and just as intense. He is such a joy to behold and has added another dimension to our happiness as a family.

While in Korea we were fortunate to visit, along with four other families, the city campus of the Korean agency which is home to children with disabilities, orphaned children, those who had not been legally relinquished for adoption, and Esther's Home for unwed mothers. I had thought a lot about visiting Esther's Home. It was something I desperately wanted to do, though I felt uncertain as to how I would cope with the reality of it. As we approached the building I began to feel that I had no right to go in. I felt humbled by those mothers who had sacrificed so much for the love of their children. Eventually, I was the only one left standing outside. With my head bowed and tears in my eyes, I slowly approached the rest of the group waiting for me in the foyer.

Inside it was so quiet, so ordered, so sorrowful. Our tour ended outside the dining room. 'The women of Esther's Home have prepared lunch for you,' our guide, Miss Kim, a social worker, said as she gestured into the near empty dining room. 'Please, do take a seat!' I walked gingerly into the room and sat at the far end of the table. Mrs Lee, the director of Esther's Home, joined our group. She sat at the head of the table, next to me. As the meal was served she began to speak of the reasons women enter the home, and how they are supported to make decisions regarding their unborn child's future. The mood at the table was sober. Mrs Lee gently peeled away the facade surrounding the reality of relinquishment and adoption. I stared deeply into her beautiful face as she spoke. Her eyes were warm and loving yet revealed the pain she had shared with many women as they grappled with life-altering, soul-destroying decisions in a culture that left them little true choice.

I turned towards my mother who was sitting beside me and glimpsed two young women, each with a tiny, heavily swaddled bundle in their arms, walking slowly down the stairs and into the foyer. Their faces were free from expression on their journey across the foyer floor and out the main entrance. They stopped beside an agency van, the door slid open, and they passed their tiny bundles into outreached arms, turned and walked back inside.

'What's happening?' I blurted out to Mrs Lee.

'Those children are on their way to Seoul, to the nursery,' she explained.'And their mothers?' I cried.

'They will be guests at a party to celebrate the new life they have given their children.'

I tried hard to quell the tears. My body ached all over. I could not fathom what I had just witnessed.

'Come and live in Australia,' I wanted to scream. 'You can keep your baby, and save yourself the misery of a life without them.'

Back at the guest house in Seoul, I thought of the two little babies who had just joined 30 or so others in the nursery earlier that day. And I thought of their mothers, whose pain would last a lifetime, undermining every happiness, never fading, always enduring. Enduring . . .

I can endure anything if it is for your happiness, my dear. I can endure anything if it is for your good future. As my mother used to say, this is the way for you . . .

Every day I am thankful for the privilege of being called 'Mummy' by two amazing, intelligent and beautiful children. I accept in my heart that my children each have three mothers who love them. I try to be the best mother I can be every moment of every day. This is the pledge I make to the other mothers. This is my life's purpose, for I have been truly blessed.

Adopting Min

Marilyn Jacobs

Finally the adoption agency rang. At last! We had been matched with a child, a six-year-old girl from an orphanage in Udonthani, a town in the north of Thailand. Her name was Pakjira, later she would become known by her Thai nickname, Min. We were asked to come into the agency to view the photograph of Min and to skim the two-page report on the child and decide if we wanted to proceed with the adoption. The photo was a very small snapshot and I could barely see what she looked like. The report on the other hand was great, no obvious problems. She was described as a lovely girl, sociable and happy.

We requested a day to ensure our decision was the right one. This request was granted. We just needed that small transition time to adjust to the fact that it was really going to happen. A couple of years of interviews, workshops, adoption agency formalities, documentation and numerous cheques were now transforming into the delightful reality that we were going to be the parents of a beautiful little girl. Ivars, my husband, was jubilant. I, too, was elated and could only liken my feelings to those of a woman in pregnancy within weeks of childbirth. Truly, it was just like that – being pregnant; within a few weeks we would be doting parents. At work I floated around showing Min's photo and sharing my excitement.

We frantically finished Min's new bedroom, purchased the toys and estimated what would be needed or required. I spoke to people endlessly about the developmental stage of a six-year-old. I didn't have a clue, having had no exposure to young children. We practised pronouncing her name, collated a survival list of

Thai words, and eagerly anticipated someone special about to come into our lives. We secured flights, accommodation in Bangkok and Udon, and finalised trip details. Then came the travel to Thailand to meet our child and bring her home. Nothing could have been simpler and nothing more exciting than the anticipation of this.

Our first contact with Min was at the Udon orphanage. After a warm reception with the orphanage director, Sarima, we were kindly escorted down a few short, wet, muddy tracks to the some-what basic classrooms dotting the orphanage site. It all had the flavour of a 1970s public school. We were ushered to the open doorway of a classroom totally unaware that this was Min's recep-tion room. Upon our arrival, the teacher instructed a few of the children to sing and dance a rehearsed song for us.

At this point it was my husband who recognised Min dancing in the middle of a single line of six girls while the remaining children sat attentively at their desks. I didn't immediately make the connection that the one child who stood out from the others was the very child we were to adopt. She was a spectacularly attractive girl and there was an unusual quality about her. When I realised it was Pakjira, I was ecstatic. After the girls' performance we approached her gently and warmly. She seemed a little distant; to us it was a simple case of initial shyness.

After giving Min a small, brown teddy bear we participated in some of the classroom activity, taking the opportunity to observe her, look at her workbooks, drawings and so on. We directed her to distribute from the suitcase we were carrying the numerous toys we had brought for the other children. Min chose a gold bead bracelet and, sustaining a very reserved demeanor, quietly distrib-uted the remaining gifts to her classmates. I could sense that she was only tolerating us at this stage. We had been informed, however, that Min had been prepared for our visit, the adoption process had been explained to her, and she was quite familiar with the small album of our home photographs sent many months before. In fact, she had the album with her and there was no doubt she was expecting us. We looked through the photos together and she seemed interested, particularly in the cats photographed in cute positions. Yet still she remained reserved, perhaps even wary of us. After a look at her school workbooks, we all moved outside of the classroom to an adjacent playground. Following a short stint watching her in the playground, looking at the chooks and attempting to keep the atmosphere as unthreatening as possible, Min and her classmates lined up before two huge cauldrons of rice and soup for lunch before we headed back, together, to Sarima's office.

When we reached Sarima's reception area, Min's wariness turned to anguish. Uncontrollable tears began to fall. She did not want to go and she did not want to go with us. Her distress was very painful due to her limited understanding of what adoption meant. Sarima's attempts to console Min were fruitless but our firm resolve, mutually shared by Sarima, was to take Min to the hotel at this point and begin the adjustment process in a new environment. As we sat in the reception area waiting for our transport to arrive, Min continued to cry. She would not look at us, showing clear mistrust. The tears just kept flowing. It was so disheartening to see her fearful face full of apprehension and anxiety. To her it must have been formidable, two strangers who not only looked different but also sounded different. We were taking her away and she knew that. She recoiled from our attempts to comfort and console her. In preparing for her departure, Sarima gave her a small bag as a farewell gift. Her only personal possessions were her schoolbooks, album and teddy, and the clothes and shoes she was wearing.

Time went slowly as we waited for the orphanage van, driven by David, to come and collect us. We felt awkward, embarrassed at not knowing how to deal with this and above all, totally helpless. Finally our driver arrived and Min, accompanied by a social worker, reluctantly had to climb in. I felt a gnawing sickness in my stomach as her crying intensified. I knew that this child for some time was going to be inconsolable and that we, as parental novices, were at a loss about what to do.

When we arrived at the hotel, the social worker went to work to help settle Min. It was a huge task for Min to cope emotionally with the move from the orphanage to the hotel. As part of the adjustment process, our week in that hotel was to be broken up by regular visits from Min's orphanage friends to help ease her in more gently. At least that was the theory.

Once everyone had left us to settle in by ourselves, the experience became even more painful. This poor child was lost, scared and overwhelmed. To express this she changed her crying into a resonating wail that was constant and endless. She began calling out pathetically for her now invisible friends. She just stood at the window, wailing and calling the names of the ones she loved. She clearly perceived us as threatening, taking her from her orphanage family. From this point, we knew she was suffering intense grief. She desperately wanted the orphanage; she needed to be back with her friends. No matter what preparation she may have had – photos and explanations of adoption – nothing impacted more than the simple fact that she knew she was being wrenched from everything familiar and safe. This she clearly understood. Because of us, her protective cocoon had prematurely burst open and I felt part of a process that increasingly resembled an act of cruelty.

Min's intense grief and constant wailing were a wrench in the gut. Nothing we could do or say could alleviate her intense distress. Most of the day she stood at the hotel window, a thin, forlorn figure, arms outstretched on the glass, her eyes looking for a sign, a hope, a miracle that someone from out there would come and get her, rescue her from our supposedly evil clutches and return her to safety. The pathos in her wailing was her recognition of the fact that she no longer had a choice. The screaming was her act of defiance, her vain attempt to exercise an influence on the choice that others had made for her.

But her choice to be returned to her home was lost, almost. I have to admit I had moments of intense doubt. I was wavering, questioning the morality and feasibility of what we were doing. I was collapsing within my own distress and inability to cope, toying with the notion of failure. It just seemed far too cruel. Perhaps we were incompatible? Perhaps it was wrong of us to remove her from the only security she had, just to satisfy our own desires to have a child? It was quite overwhelming, almost unbearable, living though someone else's pain. Ivars seemed to be more in control in this respect. Should we give in and return her to the orphanage and return home alone? The decision was already made. We were there and we couldn't pull out. We had to deal with our anxiety and most importantly, help Min deal with hers.

My husband later admitted that he had less doubt; he simply kept her long-term future in sight. He knew she would be better off. He did not like the wailing but hadn't been surprised by it.

We attempted an outing in Udonthani, the local shopping centre. Robinsons, around the corner from the hotel, was an American three-storey shopping complex including a children's entertainment area with rides and the like. Min went on one ride and for the first time I glimpsed a split-second smile. But even in a children's arena, she was still not comfortable. After the ride she began to cry, creating a public commotion and forcing us to reluctantly return to the confines of the hotel. Ivars had to carry her back despite the handfuls of hair she was attempting to yank from his head. She struggled frantically, attempting to free herself from his grip, screaming out words in Thai to attract public attention. Concerned locals looked on suspiciously. Our Thai word for adoption did, thankfully, work wonders, exonerating us from the suspicion that we may have in fact been attempting a child abduction. Perhaps in Udonthani, the locals are used to this: Westerners, like ourselves, collecting long-awaited children. Although we were within minutes of our hotel, we had little choice but to hail a nearby *tuk-tuk* as the screaming and Ivar's bruising worsened. It was hot, it was embarrassing, and it was stressful. Our arrival back at the hotel was both a retreat from public scrutiny and an enforced imprisonment.

Even in the hotel room, we weren't safe. Min threw saucers and plates in the kitchen area. We were fortunate enough to have an executive suite and boy did we need that extra space. At night, it wasn't much better. She didn't sleep much and we could hear her pathetic whimpering from her bed, a mattress on the floor. She refused to sleep in the single bed provided. During the day, television did calm her a little. Foxtel was a godsend; wall-to-wall cartoons that temporarily distracted her from her misery.

To try to lighten her transition, we asked the orphanage personnel to bring her friends over for a little party. We had cordial and cookies brought to the room, the kids watched cartoons and ran around the hotel grounds, paddled in the swimming pool and looked at the fish-pond. Min's spirits seemed to pick up a little, but unfortunately it was only temporary. Being reunited with her friends possibly ignited within her a false hope that her stay with us was to end. As we expected, once the party was over, her sense of abandonment heightened and her distress returned full force.

A further trip to a market near the Mekong River, then to Nong-Kai to see the ancient statues helped, particularly with the assistance of the assigned social worker. She was very sweet, but her accent made communication difficult. This lead to the recruitment of an English- and Thai-speaking Belgian woman who helped us enormously. These short outings distracted Min briefly, but once back in the hotel room, the tears resumed. At one point, her teacher stood outside the door and listened. Min's crying and intense grief reduced her to tears.

Min's final interaction with her friends and teacher was at the airport. A small group came to say goodbye. She was reserved, restrained and very quiet. I knew she was hoping we would hop on the plane without her. Despite all the reinforcing from Thai adults that she was going to start a new life in Australia and find happiness, it was something she couldn't accept. Even the hairdresser at the hotel spent a long time with Min explaining to her that her life would be wonderful. But here, at the Udon airport, was stark reality. The time to board triggered another defiant eruption and we had to literally drag her on the plane, Ivars suffering more biting and hair pulling.

Once on the plane, Min settled a little, knowing there was no turning back to the waving arms and smiling faces of her little friends. The flight attendants were a godsend, entertaining her throughout the flight. In fact, she spent very little time with us. We were heading to Bangkok to stay one more week. In retrospect, that week ended up being an eternity. It would have been better had we booked a flight more or less straight home.

The Bangkok phase of our journey was intensely emotional. Not only were we sick and run down with an infection, but Min's unrelenting distress continued to confine us to life in either the hotel foyer or our room. In the hotel, she latched on to anyone Thai whether they were hotel cleaners, guests or staff. Gone were our visions of sharing a fun holiday with a cute little girl. Gone were the visions of wandering around sight-seeing, shopping and eating out. And gone was any sense that the adoption process was a joyful experience. Our life as a new family was one of enforced confinement. Thankfully the staff were very supportive and understanding, both in Bangkok and Udon. But language barriers didn't help and Min capitalised on this, befriending staff within range in her attempt to find an escape. She even tried making phone calls from the hotel.

It was at this stage that we detected a slight easing of the wailing and chanting, though she would still call out the names of people she missed. Once she thought she saw the orphanage director in the street 15 floors below our hotel room. She took my husband for a walk, looking for Sarima in the Bangkok streets. There, she told strangers she wanted to go home. We were fearful she would run away and had to watch her closely.

We also had to come to terms with the sense of rejection we were feeling. She rejected our attempts to touch or cuddle her in any way. She withdrew at our every attempt to console her. For help and personal support, we faxed our concerns to friends who knew a psychiatrist, and received information that Min was suffering a profound separation anxiety and that she would regress, probably profoundly, for the immediate term. They suggested we see a doctor and ask for sedatives to help reduce her anxiety temporarily, and ours too. Lollies as a positive reinforcer were also suggested. Phone calls from the adoption agency in Australia and our friends drove home similar messages: *stick with it . . . bring her home no matter what . . . her reaction is normal . . . it will all pass . . . stay on track . . . support each other . . . and don't take things too personally*. Whatever positive and encouraging communication we received from Australia, we clung to. We were in a strange country with little support and needed that distant direction just to keep going. We knew Min needed more time and that the wailing and tantrums would dilute. The agency reassured us that we would have greater control once home on our own territory. In the meantime it was suggested we try to increase Min's sense of control. They would organise a social worker as additional support once we returned home.

The tantrums were most definitely to test us. When I communicated to Min she was a 'good girl', she replied '*Mai dec dee*' ('Not good girl'), and deliberately spilt her drink on the hotel carpet. She would do other defiant things like scribble over our drawings and urinate on the hotel carpet, her agenda being that if she presented herself as a difficult child we would willingly take her back to Udon. This became even more obvious when, as we reinforced that as her new mummy and daddy we still loved her even when she was naughty, she expressed extreme anger. At least she was releasing emotion rather than withdrawing totally. We guessed that was the healthier behaviour, but it did take its toll on us. We had no idea that the adoption process could be this emotionally draining.

Over the two weeks in Thailand, we did observe subtle changes. Although the wailing continued, the tantrums were becoming less frequent, less intense and less prolonged. We then had the next hurdle to surmount, that delicate balance of managing grief reactions versus plain naughtiness. It was there we let her have control. Discipline was simply inappropriate, if not cruel. No matter what she did, we vigorously sustained a caring manner, reaching out where we could. Minor progress occurred. Her eye contact with us was increasing and she watched our movements more closely, but cuddling and hugging was out of the question. The only way we could touch her was in an incidental way such as a passing stroke or a quick pat, and through daily routines like brushing her hair. It hurt but we understood she needed to build her trust in us. To her, we were a huge threat and she needed to learn for herself and in her own way about who we were and why we were to be in her life. Yes, we had set the initial terms; she was to be in our lives and in our country. But, she also needed to set her terms in response to our wrenching her from security and familiarity. She wasn't a two-year-old relatively oblivious to change. She was a six-year-old who understood that her life was undergoing a major shift from the institutionalised care upon which she had come to depend. At this delicate emotional stage, all we could hope for was a small sign – a smile, a look of acceptance, anything to indicate to us that perhaps she could accept us. That was still yet to happen.

PS from Min:

Dear Mum and Dad,

I wish I knew, back then, what wonderful parents you were to be for me because then I would not have cried that much. I deeply regret how much anguish I have caused you. Without your patience I would probably have never known this wonderful life in Australia, a life with such loving parents. Thank you for your greatest gift to me – yourselves. Perhaps one day I might also write my own personal version of being adopted from another country.

Love Min XXOO

A long way home

Jo-Anne Duffield

It is New Year's Eve 2002, and after a long flight from Kuala Lumpur, Adelaide is in sight. The pilot announces that the weather conditions are hazardous. Fantastic. We have been all the way to India and back and the conditions in *Adelaide* are hazardous! The wind is whipping around the plane and we are belted up for a shaky landing.

As we are all struggling off the plane, I look through tears at my mum, who has been our strength for the last 21 days. 'Three of us departed, six of us have returned. We have done it.' The look on her face is one of total relief.

But it is not over. The wait in customs is lengthy. The children are becoming increasingly restless and confused. While we wait I decide to dress the girls in their traditional Indian clothes. They look beautiful and are ready to meet their new family and friends. The customs officials, sensing our frustration, take pity on us. We are cleared ahead of the others.

Before we know it we are being greeted by our family and friends. I have never been so proud, so relieved, so exhausted, and so emotional, all at the same time. There is not a dry eye. The time has come to introduce our beautiful children: five-year-old Anita, Sophie, three, and Lucy, a tiny 16-month-old. Our Indian adventure is finally over. Our next big adventure is to get the girls home to Crystal Brook, a 200-kilometre drive from Adelaide in a car with seat belts.

Before we left for India I had organised a car seat for Lucy to be fitted to our car. It was a bit tricky, not really knowing her size, but I took an educated guess. I thought I planned our homecoming down to the very last detail but I had forgotten to ask how to buckle Lucy into the car seat. Consequently she sleeps most of the way home in my arms. Anita and Sophie nervously chat away to each other in their own Marathi language. They communicate with us mainly through sign language.

Home at last, another emotional and challenging time for us. We explain to the girls that this is their new home, but their understanding is limited. They are confused and scared.

It is really hard to say goodbye to Mum. Even though she lives just down the road we will miss her constant loyal support and her continuous encouragement. I wish Mum could stay with us for our first night home, our first time caring for our new family alone. But she needs to rest and it is time for her to go home with Dad. It has been a tough 21 days for him and a lonely Christmas without his wife.

While we were in India we all shared the same room and the girls the same bed. Wherever we went we made their bed up on the floor and they were content to be all together.

We introduce the girls now to their new bedroom, pointing to their different beds. They don't have to respond in words, the horror in their big brown eyes says it all. So we set up a mattress on the floor and explain that their mummy and daddy will sleep in the same room in their beds. By this time Stephen and I are beyond tired. Anita and Sophie are safely asleep together on the mattress on the bedroom floor but Lucy is proving difficult. After a couple of frustrating hours I finally realise we haven't fed her. With all the confusion over where to sleep we have forgotten to feed our baby! After feeding her, she falls asleep and we put her in her cot.

Stephen and I sleep in the girls' room for the first week while Anita and Sophie continue to sleep on the floor. I stay for a couple more nights before I feel I can leave them and a few nights later they hesitantly climb into their own beds. We leave their bed made up on the floor but they don't return to it.

It isn't long before our families unite in our back yard, happily playing with our new daughters. This is the moment I've been dreaming about for a long time. Anita, Sophie and Lucy are greeted with love, acceptance, affection and . . . with gifts. These little girls have never seen so many toys!

After seven years of heartache with IVF and three years on the adoption rollercoaster we are all home. I have lived in this small country town in the Mid North of South Australia all my life and Stephen grew up on a farm nearby. The whole community has waited anxiously with us for our beloved girls, riding the emotional highs and lows. Over the next few days the constant flow of friends bearing gifts for the girls and meals for us is appreciated but very tiring. Our girls are treated like celebrities, everyone wanting to see them and spend time getting to know them. Stephen and I are constantly told how lucky we are and how beautiful our girls are and we feel proud to be a part of such a friendly town. But our girls need time to bond with us, they need time to explore their new home and surroundings, and they need time to themselves to absorb all the dramatic changes that are happening in their lives. We need some time to be alone together.

Our girls start to realise that this is a safe place to be, a place where strangers are kind to them. But it doesn't take long for our perfect bubble to burst. Stephen wakes one morning with a high temperature and a rash. With help from a dear friend he is rushed to hospital. We have had all the recommended vaccinations for travelling to India but we are taking no chances.

Stephen is finally diagnosed with chickenpox. I am panic-stricken. I have a sick husband who cannot lift his head off his pillow and three children with whom I can barely communicate, much less care for. They demand every minute of my attention. I am exhausted. I beg Stephen through my tears to get out of bed and help me as I am not managing on my own.

News of Stephen's chickenpox travels fast and there are no more visitors. The days are long, the weather is hot, and the children don't understand why Daddy is in bed and Mummy is crying all the time.

My childhood friend Alex rescues me. She ignores the fact that Stephen has a contagious illness and arrives each morning with high expectations of a very busy day – and we never let her down!

She supports me in all aspects of parenting and allows me the time to care for my sick husband. She only leaves after the children have been fed and bathed at night.

After three weeks Stephen recovers enough to return to work. This is hard. All I ever wanted was to be a mother and here I am alone with these three little girls, our daughters, and I am supposed to be happy and fulfilled. Instead I feel unhappy and worn out.

I cry a lot. Adopting three children at once is a lot harder than I ever imagined. I wonder if we have done the right thing. I never question my love for the girls but it is all too much at times. Everywhere I go I am followed. I am in constant demand. There is so much extra washing and ironing and I am constantly picking up toys. Every minute is spent tending the children and no amount of counselling could have prepared me for these negative feelings.

Day by day, Anita and Sophie's English improves – I am amazed at how quickly they begin to comprehend their new language – and Lucy has started to crawl, which makes things easier. We spend as much time as we can outside. The girls have a swing set and mini trampoline and have been given bikes. We discover Anita and Sophie are very uncoordinated. We know that after 16 months in an orphanage with little stimulation their legs have become thin and weak and lack muscle tone. We spend hours teaching and encouraging and eventually they can swing themselves and ride their bikes with the aid of training wheels. The trampoline helps them to balance. I am still struggling with the lack of time for myself, but things are improving.

We have been home for six weeks and it is time for Anita to go to kindergarten. She is old enough to go to school but we think her development will benefit from starting initially at kindy. We obtain special permission for this. The kindy also organises one-on-one teaching for Anita.

The first day is heart-breaking. I leave my daughter screaming at the gate, totally traumatised, and cry all the way home to Mum's. I ring the kindy several times and cannot wait until lunch time to pick her up. What a relief – she appears to be enjoying herself!

After that first day kindy is fantastic. It doesn't take long for Anita to look forward to Tuesdays and Thursdays and she is learning at a rapid rate. She loves her support teacher and has made some friends, communicating with them under the teacher's watchful eye. Anita still needs to be reminded of simple things like going to the toilet but between our attention at home and that of her teacher at kindy, we think Anita is ready for school.

Anita starts Reception at Crystal Brook Primary School but finds the transition from kindy to school really difficult. She can't seem to settle down in a more structured environment and sitting and listening for extended lengths of time prove too hard for her. Her teacher has transferred from kindy to school to be with her which is a comfort to us.

The only time we face antipathy is when we travel to other towns. We look different from other families in South Australian country towns. We are asked: *Are they yours? Do they call you Mum and Dad? Are they real sisters?* – often in front of the children. This hurts me the most. I always take the time to explain our situation and answer the questions but I make sure people understand that I feel these are sensitive issues and hope they will consider the children's feelings in future.

Anita begins to make progress. She learns her ABC, counts to one hundred, writes her name, address and telephone number and identifies her colours. We are very proud parents indeed. Life seems to be going smoothly. Anita appears settled at school, Sophie has started playgroup and is making new friends and little Lucy is attempting to walk. I am thinking just maybe I'll make a parent yet when I am reminded how fragile we all still are.

Anita is being bullied at school. She is too afraid to tell anyone and it only comes to a head when it is witnessed by a teacher. She is being kicked and punched. This is a real turning point in my short time as a parent. I am horrified that someone is kicking and punching my child and an over-protective side of me is born. From that moment on, anyone messes with my children, they mess with me!

The school's anti-bullying procedure ensures the other child involved is dealt with but we feel it offers little for the victim.

I decide to take matters into my own hands. I contact a friend who is a kindergarten director and ask for help. She has a brilliant book which explains bullying in children's terms. For the next few nights, Stephen and I read to Anita. Soon she is convinced she isn't doing anything wrong and that it isn't her fault she is being picked on.

The distress of bullying recedes but there are more challenges. As the eldest child, Anita has always felt responsible for her sisters; she has mothered them since she was four. There has been no opportunity for her to be a little girl while caring for and protecting her siblings, before and during their time in the orphanage. And now she feels I am trying to replace her biological mother, or maybe even her. She resents me as a threat to her relationship with her sisters. I explain that Sophie and Lucy need to start their new life and learn to do things for themselves, but she ignores me and continues to do everything for her sisters. This is, of course, admirable in its way but the tension between us continues to grow. I want my girls to be little girls; to play, to have fun, to smile. After several weeks it comes to a head. I rebuke Anita for some minor incident and she loses control and yells and screams at me. I am hurt when she tells me I am not her real mother. How can I be when I am not brown? She seems quite pleased with herself when she sees me cry and I am overwhelmed. Nothing has prepared me for this! I thought this sort of behaviour might rear its ugly head in adolescence, not when she is five. I am so angry and hurt that I decide it is best not to react.

Stephen and I both cry a lot of tears over this incident. I am really struggling but I continue to try to be the best mother I can. I ring our social worker for advice on how to handle another outburst, should it happen again. Just as well. The next time it happens I am ready. I respond to Anita's claims that I am not her real mother by holding her tight. I agree that I am not her real mother but tell her that I am the only one she has got and that I love her dearly and that we are both here to stay; that this is her new home and we are a family and that Sophie and Lucy are staying as well. I tell her that I am mother to them all and that I have to be shared. This is uncomfortable for us both but is a significant moment in our relationship.

I also make an appointment to see a psychologist who calls himself 'the worry doctor'. I am unprepared for Anita's response as she opens up to this stranger, telling him all her worries and the problems associated with living in a new country and having a new mother. Both Anita and I cry freely and I wish Stephen could share this.

I am deeply affected by what Anita is saying. I realise I have been busy with the demands of a new family and consumed with the adoption. I have been selfishly considering all that *I* had to give up to be a mother and have felt jealous of Stephen escaping the day-to-day running of this frantic house by going to work while I am stuck home. I sit listening to our dear little girl pour her heart out to a complete stranger and I realise how much more she has given up than me. Stephen and I have taken these girls from the orphanage and given them a second chance at life but we have not understood how much they miss India. Anita misses her friends at the orphanage and she misses her other family.

We only need one visit. The psychologist has given Anita and me a powerful message and we have not looked back. She is still slowly learning to be a child and I am forever learning to be the best mother I can. No, I don't always get it right.

Anita, Sophie and Lucy are the only adopted sibling group in Crystal Brook. We really don't think the colour of their skin is an issue for others, though sometimes their ignorance or curiosity comes through. We have always told our girls to be proud of their beautiful brown skin, and we believe they are. Education is the key to understanding and I have spent a lot of time explaining to Anita, Sophie and Lucy how and why they now live in Australia and why they have a new mummy and daddy. I find that everyone, adults and children alike, appreciate our honesty.

Stephen has been a tower of strength. It was never his idea to adopt and it took some talking before he came around. When we received photos before we went to India, I would be excited like any expectant mother and he would be rather reserved. He organised all the adoption paperwork as I found it confusing. All I wanted was to go to India and collect our children. Friday 13 December 2002, unlucky for some but the luckiest day of our lives. Stephen was smitten the moment he laid eyes on his girls and has been ever since.

Our lives have certainly changed for the better. Being a parent is hard work but rewarding. There is never a dull moment and parenting three very active children with distinctly different personalities has its challenges. But we are firm believers that life is all about opportunities and beginnings. We made a promise and a commitment to our daughters, and it is one we take very seriously. It's been a long way home.

Birth parents —
a part of our family

Louise Gale

Dear . . .
As I gaze at your son's photograph in front of us, I think of you. Perhaps you now know he is joining a family in Australia.

I think about what he is doing in Seoul waiting for us, growing with his foster family and knowing at this time this is something we share. We are waiting to meet him for the first time and bring him into our family and you are waiting, hoping your pain will become less and hoping he will be happy. I cannot begin to imagine what you are thinking or how you are coping. Writing this I have tears running down my face. I want to be able to tell you that we will love him forever, I want to show you that you are in our hearts though we have never met you. We are truly humbled that we are able to be parents through adoption; I do not know what it is like to have a child grow in my body, only in my heart.

All of us in life are looking for love and acceptance and you have a broken relationship and a son you will not raise. I know you cared for him deeply for he is so beautiful and healthy. I am sorry that his father could not help you to care for him — your bravery and courage is heartbreaking. Your son is not lost. Though he will not grow up in Korea, he will not be alone: he has a brother who is five years old and a sister who is three years old. They, like him, were born in Korea and adopted.

For us he has already brought so much joy, his brother and sister cannot wait to meet him and have helped prepare his clothes and toys. He will always know that you gave him life and loved him and wanted him to have a family. You are part of our family in our hearts.

If there is any information we can share with you or if you would like photographs we are more than willing to send these to you as you have allowed us to share your son. We have travelled each time to Korea to bring our children home and will travel regularly so that they may know their birthplace.

May you find peace and happiness in your life. We promise to care for him and tell him of you with respect and love. Korea is a part of our souls and always in our thoughts.

With love . . .

What do you say when meeting a birth mother? *Thank you* does not feel right, but neither does *goodbye*. *Welcome to our family* feels more appropriate but even that may be thwarted by language, distance and culture. But for me, birth parents are family.

Our first two children were relinquished at birth following concealed pregnancies. I have sent letters and photos to Korea to keep on file so that their birth mothers may one day know how and where their children are. Each time I have reiterated that we are always willing to share information, the birth mother only need ask. Even if we never hear, it would be comforting to learn that they know their children are an adored part of our family. We will not search for their birth mothers, for we believe that is our children's choice when they are adults.

Our third child, a son, was cared for by his birth mother with the help of a friend for the first two weeks of his life. She realised that it was an impossible dream to keep him. Soon after allocation I wrote a letter to her through the agency, to be given to her or left on file depending on whether she contacted the agency. Six weeks after allocation we were told she had been in touch with the intake worker and had decided to meet us. We were aware that it was still another few weeks before we would be in Korea and that she could change her mind.

On the Tuesday we met our son for the first time, our social worker was trying to contact the birth mother's intake worker to ascertain whether she still wished to meet us. On Wednesday we were told that we were to meet her the following day.

It was a much greater risk for her to meet us than vice versa. For us the whole process, including meeting our new baby, as we had done twice before, was still surreal. Moreover there were no cultural stigmas for us. With our first two children, it was not until we were home for a few days that it began to feel real. Our son's birth mother's courage and strength, to not only meet us but to bring a friend with her, was testament to the love she maintains for her son.

Prior to meeting her I was filled with mixed emotions. Would she like us? Were we good enough? Did I look all right? Would she want him back?

She wanted and still wants him in her life, but she realised that culturally and economically she could not care for him. This reality has meant that he is with us. Of course the anxiety was not one-sided. We both admitted that we had not slept the night before because of nerves. Though it was awkward – she was obviously upset and much was lost in translation – I believe for her it was a closure and a beginning. She knew that once she had said goodbye the first time she did not have the right to see her son again. As a result of our request to meet her she was allowed to see him again, and she thanked us for that chance. I had always thought naively that, as in Australia, his mother could see him as often as she liked once he was placed in foster care. But his birth place and his foster placement were hours apart, as they were for our other two children.

In some ways seeing us was a comfort for her. It made her 'feel more at peace with her decision' she told us through an interpreter, knowing who her son would live with and where he was going. She said it lessened her guilt. She was so brave, holding back tears from her red and swollen eyes. She had vacillated in her decision to meet us; she would see her son again but it meant another goodbye. He looks like her, and I was shattered as I looked at her holding him, hugging him a last time before she gave him to me. I then gave him to his foster mother for another few days before we returned home. I had remained composed until that moment, not wanting to lose control, knowing that I do not quietly shed tears but rather gasp for breath. It is that moment I remember the most of the whole meeting.

She had been told we were a 'nice family', active in the adoption community. We think we are just average and we told her that. I did not want her to think that we believe we are better than her. It is certainly not because we are better than her that her son joins our family but a result of the social, cultural and economic differences of the countries in which we live. She was able to question us about what type of house we live in and what type of Korean things we do in our family. We reiterated that we would always love her son, talk of her, and share any news that she chose to share with us. She asked for monthly updates. I had to tell her that with three children I could not promise monthly updates but that I would forward photos as we had them developed and I would write two to three times a year.

How will our son's two siblings react to the absence of photos and links with their own birth parents? We wonder if we should have bypassed this experience for our third child because our first two children do not have the links. But I don't think so. We don't know what the future holds. In the meantime we will continue to give them all as much information as possible and share with them as much of our understanding of the culture. We know openness and information sharing is not always possible.

What did I learn through this process? That humanity crosses all borders. One of the concerns I have along with other parents is that our children's birth parents were coerced. More through cultural undercurrents but not, I believe, through pressure from professionals we have met in Korea. Those with whom they came into contact through the relinquishing process and those we met appeared genuinely supportive and compassionate. I don't want our children to see their birth parents as victims to whom they owe nothing, nor do I want them to feel a burden of debt to us. I hope that through this contact we can gain insight for all three of our children.

This second letter was written five weeks after arriving home.

Dear . . .
Perhaps you are wondering after meeting us how our baby, yours and mine, is faring? I know meeting us was a very hard decision for you to make. As I said when we met, he is a credit to you. He is healthy and beautiful because of the care you gave yourself while he grew within you. I can only

promise that we too will try to give him, together with his brother and sister, the things they need to allow them to blossom into adults that any parent would be proud of. We will instil a sense of pride in their Korean birthplace and respect for those who share their children with us.

He laughs and babbles as he crawls, looking for something else to put in his mouth, looking back occasionally to check if he is still being watched or whether he is free to escape into another room and perhaps find something else more inviting. His sister cannot keep from cuddling him, telling us regularly, 'I love him, he is wonderful.' He has added a dimension to our family that is truly magic, his brother so very proud to tell and show all his school friends his new brother, sharing all his accomplishments: new teeth, rolling, sitting and blowing raspberries. If he does not know now how much he is adored and loved he will grow into it through the years.

Since seeing and sharing your tears and grief in saying goodbye to him a second time I have found it hard to see the rainbow as I think of your sadness. But as you said, coming into our family is a celebration. It is not that we are perfect by any means but that through the masses of legal documentation and emotion he now has two families. In his smile I see your face, your courage and all that he will be.

I hope now that you know where he is you can be happy in life and share your life with someone special. It is heartening to know that you have such good friends and family who have supported you over the last year.

Thinking of you . . .

Adoption theorists talk about the triad of loss that continues through adoption and life and I do not contest that as individuals we all experience loss throughout our lives. Infertility for us was merely one door closing and another opening. I have experienced other losses that were far more powerful and significant than infertility. Though I can only speak for our family, we have gained immeasurable joy and love through our adoption journeys so far, and our children and their birth cultures have given us more than we could have ever imagined. Not only are we now parents, an obvious plus, but we have added another dimension to our lives through another culture. It has given us new directions and hope and a much broader perspective of the wider issues of humanity and community.

Our three children are all exceptional, but what mother wouldn't say that of her children? Much of their beauty is due to the foundation they received while in the care of their birth mothers and reflected in their innate natures. Only a limited few of us are privileged to have been able to meet their children's birth mother. We were given this gift.

Forensic astrology

Melina Magdalena

I remember waking up at five one morning, my face wet with tears, return of memory making my heart beat faster. I had another brother whom I had abandoned and forgotten. It was nine years ago and I was 25. I still have dreams where I wake up with the panic of having lost something precious, but not knowing what or who.

I am an early riser, just like my mother. I used to get up at 5 am when I was still at school. My mother and I were connected, we were alike, we understood one another. My mother and I, both born under the sign of Pisces, swam against the steamy tide of fire and air, signs to which everyone else in our family belonged. In my twenties I was beginning to realise that our enmeshment was not always desirable, but it was something I had always taken for granted.

My brother had been, so the story goes, abandoned on a bus. The driver found him lying on a seat when he finished work for the day and took him to an orphanage. This was the seventh of April, year unclear. The seventh of April was thus declared to be his birthday, placing him under the fiery and impulsive sign of Aries, like our sister. The authorities could tell us nothing about where he came from, how old he really was, or how he had come to be on that bus. Due to his general physical development, our parents were later forced to revise his age up two years. This means that rather than having been found on a bus as an infant, my brother was a small child at the time, capable of language and memory. What he eventually told us about where he had come from makes me weep for everything he lost – far more than just his birth date.

The orphanage was in Manila. My brother never talked about it much, except to say that the girls did all the work, and he had Coke to drink all the time. These issues engendered an immediate culture clash between my brother and the rest of the family. Luckily, once the rotted baby teeth disappeared from his gums, his adult teeth grew in strong and white. In the orphanage he was called Boyett (little boy). The date recorded as his birthday was also our great grandfather's birthday, so he was given Papa's name as his first name. He got to keep Boyett as a middle name, but once he was living in Australia, no one called him that again. By doing so now, I reclaim one portion of his former identity in my thoughts about him.

In the late 1970s it wasn't unusual in a certain sector of middle-class Australian society for families to choose adoption as a method of extending their families as well as giving the chance of a better life to an orphaned child. Our parents, idealistic and warm-hearted, wanted no distinctions to be made between their five children. They were determined that we would all grow up as one happy family.

By the time Boyett came to live with us, the configuration of our family was thus: I was ten (biological); my brother was 15 months my junior (biracial, adopted at the age of three weeks); our sister (biological) was five years old and the first to be born in Australia. Boyett was said at the time to be six, one year older than our sister. Our parents had wanted to adopt a boy who would be close in age to our brother, but red tape had held up their application for years. When I was 15, our mother gave birth to another child, the fifth of the family.

I remember when our father brought Boyett back from the Phillipines. He came to our house, rugged up against the Tasmanian winter, small, forlorn, and frightened. Our parents had arranged for a Filipina to come to our home that evening to reassure him and answer any questions he had. She and her husband spoke with Boyett and our parents in the chilly living room. We children were excited and happy. Our father was home! As promised, he had brought our new brother.

According to this woman, Boyett had very little language. He didn't respond to Tagalog, Spanish or any of the other languages she tried. She suggested he had come from a remote mountain community with an indigenous language. Was he suffering an acute case of culture shock? Or perhaps he did not speak well because he had not acquired language as a small child. This matches the details of his early years that he supplied later, and hints at what was to come. One wonders at the selection process. Why was this child deemed mentally and emotionally fit to be removed from what had become his only home, to be sent away to strangers overseas? Did anyone ask him whether he wanted to come? By the time he became part of our household, Boyett had already been twice displaced.

The four of us went to a small public school. It was my job to make sure all of us went where we needed to go, before and after school. When we drove anywhere, I never got a window seat. I had to sit between my siblings to stop their back seat bickering.

We had swimming lessons at the city pool. Each week I led my brood through the streets of Hobart. A daydreamer, I was always worried that we wouldn't get there. When we eventually arrived at the gates of the pool, I abandoned myself and my responsibilities to the chlorinated blue waters for an hour of swimming, until our mother came to pick us up.

It wasn't reasonable to assume that because we were in the same family, we were of similar aptitude, attitude and interest. Within the boundaries of our family, even the expectation that we would all treat one another with respect and love seems to have been unreasonable. Not just our star sign, but our experiences determine our capacity for love and bonding. In our family there was great disparity between us.

What may seem obvious now was not clear then. Back then I was oblivious to the socio-political and intra-familial currents of conflict that damaged us all so severely. Society's nature/nurture debate played out in our family as a blame game. The fact that our adopted siblings came to us with their own histories, their own genetic memories, and their own identities was not taken into consideration. These natural differences engendered bitter conflict not so much between family members, but between our family and the outside world. Authorities and social workers designated our mother chief nurturer and therefore chief scapegoat as our family unravelled, no matter how hard she and our father worked to find ways for our family to mend and grow.

For example, when my first brother started school, he was placed with my teacher from the previous year. She assumed that he, having also been read to since he was a baby, would have taught himself to read. This was far from the case. Actually, while I had earnestly applied myself to a preschool study of nature and books, my brother had devoted his early years to attaining an advanced level of ball skills that I envied but did not resent.

My first brother and I grew further and further apart. This teacher caused lifelong damage to our relationship by making me right and good and clever, and him wrong and bad and stupid. Similar conflicts flourished in the schools that Boyett and our sister attended.

We moved from Hobart to a town in Queensland two years after Boyett came to live with us. Here, the small-mindedness of the community and teachers dismantled any shreds of self-respect and new identity that he had been able to cultivate freely during his two years with us. The injustice of his different racial appearance was a source of constant irritation to him. He was certain that no one outside the family could ever understand that he belonged with us. Nor was he sure he wanted them to.

The physical differences within our family were magnified hundred-fold in this sugar town. Though I never failed to count myself in as one of the group of marked and 'othered' people, my brothers had no chance of escaping like me into the anonymity of being one white person in a crowd. The locals had no framework from which to begin to comprehend our family. Not everyone was mean-spirited, but racial tensions were already rife in the town when we arrived. We could only ride out the storm for two years until circumstances blew us to Adelaide.

We had friends in Adelaide who had two biological sons and one adopted daughter. It was wondrous to reconnect with them when we returned. Born in Pisces, a mutable watery sign, it had been natural for me to absorb the emotions of all those around me. Our return to Adelaide saved me temporarily from deep depression. We had lived in a place that condemned me for being myself. I had other layers to unpeel besides the fact that I came from a multiracial family. At the age of 14, all I could see was that there was something wrong with me. I paid little attention to what was happening to my siblings. What could I have done anyway? I had not learned to think for myself. The skills of critical analysis deemed so essential for today's young people were not yet part of my school's curriculum.

The four of us were now at four different schools, this being one way to manage our diversity. Most of us were adolescent, and not getting along terribly well. I managed by trying to be perfect. I worked diligently at my chores, practised my musical instruments conscientiously and always did my homework. Our sister behaved in much the same way. We thought our brothers deliberately tried to cause trouble, or had no talent for keeping out of trouble. I sometimes tried to save them by shifting the blame onto myself.

During our second year back in Adelaide, our parents helped me to achieve my dream of being an exchange student. They may never understand my desperate need to escape the stranglehold of my conflicted family, but I will always be grateful for their support. However, I also carry the shadow of a deep sadness within me for what occurred while I was away. Perhaps if I had not abandoned my brothers and sister, things may have turned out differently.

I left one month shy of 15. My journey began and ended in January. I stayed with a family in Europe whose daughter lived with my family from July of that year to July of the following year. Before I left, my parents told me they were having another baby in August. He would be almost six months old before I got to meet him.

When I came home, not only was there a baby in the house, sharing a room with my exchange sister, but my first brother had disappeared. I couldn't find out what had happened. He had, apparently, 'gone to live somewhere else'.

There were already so many secrets in our family. I was used to filling in the gaps of our narrative. I was told much later that there had been family counselling. It was intimated that I had attended some of the sessions, although I have no recollection of these.

My first brother was removed from the family, because authorities thought he was incapable of understanding right from wrong. This was supposed to explain his frequent indulgence in petty crime. He was placed in a correctional program, where he soon had his fellow residents wrapped around his little finger. He was banished from that place to foster care. When that didn't work out, he was placed in a house with several boys his age and house-parents who ran an extremely tight ship, where a misdemeanour by one meant punishment for all. I am told he thrived in this environment. He came back home for a while, but when he came of age he left the city. Country life seems to suit him. He works hard, plays half a dozen different sports, and comes to see us when he can. I feel though, that our relationships were never really mended. The family legend of his removal lives on unaddressed and unquestioned. I cannot tell you how he feels about it.

I had come back from Europe destined to learn seven languages and travel the globe. Home was not so much a refuge from a forbidding world, as the place where I had to bide my time. I was a social isolate, and made myself a pariah in the classroom. Self-destruction was still my ultimate private goal. Though I became aware that there was trouble with my second brother, I had detached myself from my protective role, I had other things on my mind.

Boyett was constantly in the bad books. The hole he was in grew bigger every day and it seemed like he never tried to climb out. School was a write-off. He'd always had trouble expressing himself. I don't think he had any real friends. He didn't have a part-time job or any interests outside of school, though our parents had tried for years to get him interested. He didn't pull his weight around the house. There was no part of his life that was successful. He didn't try to interact with the rest of us.

There was nothing I could do to mediate or alleviate. I tried even harder, not to show Boyett up but to distract our parents from their obsession with his faults. I found out later from our sister that he was violent towards her, but I did not know this at the time. The litany of grievances grew. He was rude and unresponsive; he was deceitful.

The situation became intolerable. By now I was 17. I plunged into my final year of school as if only my studies could save me. I was told that it was Boyett's choice to be officially 'unadopted'. Our parents had done everything they could. He went to live with another family.

I remember saying goodbye. I had no idea what was coming. Our mother summoned my sister and me to the hallway and told us that he was leaving. She told us to shake his hand and say goodbye. Numbly, I complied. He had been abandoned twice already, but this time Boyett elected to abandon us. He had a strangely triumphant look in his eyes that I recognised, but couldn't comprehend.

I haven't seen him since that day.

The social worker who took Boyett away told him that he was not to try to contact us unless we requested it. She told our parents that they were not to contact Boyett unless he requested it. For many years we left the photograph albums on the shelves, and we did not speak his name.

About two years ago Boyett made contact with our parents. They have talked on the phone many times since, but our parents still keep him at arm's length. Boyett is employed and lives alone. He is isolated and unhappy. He doesn't get along with the members of the family he was placed with, because he treated them much the way he treated our little sister.

My brother has been diagnosed with a mental illness. I don't know whether he receives regular therapy, but my understanding of the mental health system is that people receive scripts for their medication and little else in the way of support for their conditions, even when they are trauma-induced.

Boyett told me once that he had lived with his grandmother and an older brother in a little village. In my mind I see this place from knee height. I can almost see his grandmother. There is a wire fence, a dirt road. It's muddy and there are things with spiky leaves growing near the fence, mountains in the distance, and the road is steep. I can't see the house but I know it's not far off.

One day, without warning, everyone in the village disappeared. Boyett was the only one left. For a while he ate frogs and whatever else he could find. Then he got on a bus where the driver found him and took him to the orphanage.

Sometimes I wonder about forensic astrology. The idea that the time and place I was born concurrent with the constellation of the planets has had a determining factor on my personality and destiny has long been a source of comfort for me. I like to tell myself that this, too, will pass. I know that I struggle to swim upstream because it is my nature to do so.

Could the fact that my brother was so arbitrarily allocated a birth date and a name have had such catastrophic effects on his life and ours? Was there a greater hand somewhere in the universe, pulling strings to give him a chance at a different destiny? Shouldn't it be possible to divine his star sign by examining aspects of his personality and reconstructing a time line of his experiences? Would this help him to settle into his identity? I wonder who he really is. I wonder who he could have been. I wonder how his life would have turned out if he had stayed in Manila. And most of all, I wonder how our family could have loved and accepted him any more than we did.

Journey

As we came around the corner, we were greeted by 50 or more people cheering, clapping and chanting. Belete's wife and children greeted us with flowers and kisses and tears flowed from the eyes of the many women draped in their traditional white garments.

Journey of an adoptive mum

Susan Olsen

Last Saturday was our daughter's 27th birthday and we had a family lunch at home for her. It was a cheerful noisy get-together with plenty of good food and wine and a chocolate cake decorated with strawberries. Jessie had her latest boyfriend with her and she was bright and laughing. She was enjoying the company of her nana and an aunt and cousin who had come up from Sydney for the day, although missing her little boy who was with his father for the weekend. Our 23-year-old son Joe was ensconced in his bedroom with his Internet girlfriend who he had just met for the first time after years of e-mails. She had flown down from Queensland for the weekend and as far as we could tell they were getting on pretty well. My mate of 32 years was his usual calm and helpful self, and the blue heeler was sitting hopefully by the table pleading for handouts. A pleasant day in the life of a fairly typical Australian family you might think. But our family is far from typical.

I am an adoptive mother of Jessie and Joe, who are both Aboriginal, and for many years I felt I had no right to tell my story. I felt ashamed of our possible part in the tragic events of the stolen generations. My own struggles and despair seemed nothing compared to the losses of those who had had their children wrenched from them. But in more recent times another small voice has been silently screaming *how can I* not *tell my story*? How can healing or reconciliation ever truly happen unless all angles of the adoption triangle have the courage to say how life has really been for them? So here is my story as I presented it in April 2004 at the 8th Australian Adoption Conference in Adelaide.

In the telling of my story I am in no way trying to dilute or undermine the stories of loss and grief of Indigenous Australians.

I was married when I was 28 and by my early thirties, after going through the usual rigmarole of doctors, tests and operations, I found I was infertile. We wanted a family so much and adopting children seemed a valid way of forming a family. We did not have a need to adopt children who looked like us and I originally started thinking of children from other races during all the emotional media reports about Vietnam orphans being brought to Australia. This happened around the time we were about to put in our application, but after inquiring we were told it was too late to apply for Vietnamese children. We then decided that it would be better to apply for children from our own country who would therefore be closer to their own heritage and culture. At the time we were taking part in Land Rights marches and belonged to an (all-white) Land Rights support group. But we were so naïve. I did know something of Aboriginal children being taken from their families and believed that it was all in the distant past. The biggest well of trauma for me over the years, has been the growing knowledge of the anger many Aboriginal people feel about white families adopting their children.

I was working in an office when the phone call came and two days later we had a beautiful eight-week-old baby girl to care for. We caught an overnight train from Sydney to become instant parents. The hospital staff were wonderful and gave me a crash course in changing nappies, bathing and feeding. When it was time to leave we were handed a dark-eyed smiling tot, like a parcel wrapped tightly in a blanket. *Here, she's yours, now you are a mum and dad.* Then off we went in some trepidation to catch a plane home. It took me about eight months to feel like a mother. I felt as though this longed-for baby was just on loan. I felt like a babysitter when I wheeled her around the block. I had not had nine months of growing her in my womb, but it was now up to my mate and me to 'grow her up'.

We had been told at the time of adoption that our daughter's first mum, who was only 17, had asked to have her baby adopted.

She already had a two-year-old who – I think – her mother was raising.

Three years later we adopted a dear little six-week-old boy. I felt like his mum straight away, perhaps because I had had three years to practise mothering. We were told that his first mum, who had three other children, had asked that he be adopted so he could have a dad and a mum, and because her own mother was not able to help with a fourth child. At the time we believed what we were told but I wonder now if we were told the truth. For years I have allowed myself to be burdened with guilt that is sometimes dumped on adoptive parents, whether justified or not. But guilt immobilises you and cripples your spirit, keeping you stuck in the one place, going over and over the 'what ifs' and the 'if onlys'.

For the first few years we settled into being a family in Sydney. Our daughter was a delight and a handful. She was also the first grandchild and doted on by our extended family. Our little boy was the good quiet child, with a sense of the ridiculous and a great belly laugh. His presence was not at first appreciated by our lively daughter who announced, 'He's a yucky baby, take him back!' We were not sure if we would ever receive a second child, and we had only had one day's notice before bringing Joe into our family. However the two children soon accepted each other and we felt like a *real* family.

My mate and I had been keen bushwalkers and adventurers for many years. We had met in a bushwalking club and we love the wild and rugged places of Australia. We felt that we could at least give these kids a love of the bush and a relationship to wilderness areas, albeit it a white relationship. We also wanted to form relationships with Aboriginal people and for the first few years we took part in the annual march in Sydney for what was then called National Aboriginal Day. There were some other intermittent superficial contacts with Indigenous Australians over the years, but the connections we had hoped for did not eventuate. Perhaps we did not try hard enough. We often talked about Aboriginal culture as we understood it, read Dreamtime stories to the children at bedtime and tried to instil in them a pride in their Aboriginality. But it wasn't easy. With a foot in both camps for the past 26 years I have been faced with the reality of how Aboriginal people are really up against it. There is so much negativity, so much ignorance and racism out there. Still! And the hardest racism to combat is the subtle sort, the things that are said, but not said.

When Jessie was four-and-a-half and Joe 18 months old we left our small suburban home and moved to several acres of bush in the Blue Mountains. Here we lived in caravans for nearly two years while we built our own house, partly out of bush rock collected from our land. It was a slow process and the living was rough in a rather bleak climate, with no power or town water for the first six months. But it was an adventurous and exciting time that we now look back on with some nostalgia.

Not long after our move Jessie started school. I made a point of telling the school she was Aboriginal in the naïve belief that teachers would help her be proud of her heritage and herself. This unfortunately backfired with a couple of teachers, one in particular who was racist and vindictive. The school years were a struggle from start to finish with many early 'treading on eggshells' mornings. Jessie had so much anger in her. She eventually smashed nearly everything that was given to her, bit herself and left burn marks on her bedroom carpet. In between these furious outbursts she was a lively, laughing child away from school but mostly a silent subdued one in the classroom. At that time the town was not only small but also fairly small-minded and it was not easy to be accepted if you were seen as a family that was outside the norm.

I felt that the bouts of violence and other challenging behaviours were at least partly because Jessie felt different. We had been briefly prepared for difficulties in being a so-called 'mixed-race' family in a one-day seminar, just before we adopted Joe. There had been no talks before we adopted Jessie. Perhaps it was because our application file was in the wrong section for nearly two years, until I rang the department to find out what was happening, and we may have slipped through the system. However we did read quite a lot of articles and papers on inter-racial adoption recommended to us when we first applied to adopt

Aboriginal children. With hindsight though I do wonder just how capable you are of really hearing what is being said to you when you are desperately waiting for a child. I know that in our case we believed we would be able to overcome any potential problems.

As difficulties increased in raising Jessie I also wondered if there was a subconscious feeling of loss and grief associated with being separated from her birth mother. At the time I did not get much support for my worries, because *wasn't love supposed to be enough?* It was not until years later that my gut feelings were confirmed when I read *The Primal Wound* by Nancy Newton Verrier.

At times I also had feelings of being a failure as a mother and for years did not even tell my parents, who lived down the far-south coast, much of what we were going through. We battled on and tried to solve the problems ourselves. Why didn't we seek professional help? Well, in those days I did not believe I would find a social worker who could really understand our situation. I was worried that if a wrong decision was made Jessie could disappear into the system and be lost to us, and to herself, perhaps forever.

As for Joe, he continued to be mostly the good quiet child though he had his problems, too. Early in his teenage years he appeared to reject the extended family. Instead he made his own family from good friends, some of whom he had known since he was a toddler.

When Jessie was about ten, I contacted Link-Up to ask for support and three Aboriginal women came to our house to talk to both of us. I was nervous, expecting them to be antagonistic but instead they talked to me, mothers to mother. They also talked to Jessie and lent her a video. They let her know the door was open any time she wanted to come to see them.

In between the dramas and sadness there were also happy times living in the bush, outings and holidays to many national parks and beaches and visits to far-flung family and friends. I think we did succeed in giving our kids a feeling of connection with the bush, the coast and the desert. We also had the support of family and old friends over the years and I don't know what we would have done without them.

The teenage years with Jessie were a roller-coaster ride. There were many times when I felt I could not go on amongst the violence, running away, and other problems. However we believed that as long as we 'kept the door open' we would have a chance of turning her self-destructive life around. The one positive thing in her life during those years was her horse. Jessie did also eventually agree to go to the child psychologist Distance Education insisted on, before they would agree to her doing the School Certificate by correspondence. He did prove to be of some help. As for me, I was a far from calm and rational mother at times, a bit neurotic in fact, and a terrible nagger. Our marriage nearly fell apart and life was bloody awful, but we came out the other side. You do not, of course, have to be an adoptive family to have these experiences and most of us do survive and life goes on.

There are those who might say, well, you should not have adopted these children, you got what you deserved. And I would say to them that many of us make decisions and choices with the best of intentions and for what, at the time, seem the right reasons. Once you have set out along a road that later brings you many challenges you have two choices, either to give up or to stick it out. In raising Jessie we chose fight over flight because we love her.

I have also heard it said, once or twice, that adoptive mothers are not capable of being loving mothers because they have not grieved for their infertility. While not agreeing with those comments I do agree that infertility is a little-recognised grief. I know my biggest sadness is not so much that I did not give birth, but that I did not give birth to these children we have raised. It was not until I went to a counsellor in my late forties that I began to come to terms with my loss. But most of the human race has sorrows of one sort or another which they drag around after them, sometimes for years, like a Leunig bag of roosters. Yet they also mostly do their best in living their lives and in relating to, or caring for, others.

In regard to the lack of genetic connection, I think that some of us fall over ourselves trying to please our adopted kids in an effort to make up for our lack of blood ties. Or perhaps it is more a case of never being able to do enough because we cannot fill the empty well that has been left in many adoptees, by the separation from the mothers who gave them life.

In my journey there is the little picture of day-to-day living and then there is the bigger picture of Australia's true history and my position in it. During our very troubled family times the big picture became a bit lost in the struggle to just survive from day to day. Then in 1997 the big picture leapt back at us in the form of the Reconciliation Conference and all the stories of the Stolen Children. I became briefly involved by writing a letter to the *Herald* and by having a short article published. Then TV stations and magazines started ringing me up and I rushed for cover, not wanting to bring any harm to my kids and not trusting the media.

I joined a local Reconciliation group but mostly kept quiet about being an adoptive mother. The day I signed the *Sorry Book* I was a mess. My hand moved unsteadily across the page and I had trouble holding back the tears while the keeper of the book hovered worriedly over me. The day I walked over the Harbour Bridge for Reconciliation of black and white Australians, however, was an uplifting experience. It was a vote for people power, although it did little to change the views of politicians with hearts of stone and minds set in concrete.

Jessie and Joe both now have their original birth certificates but so far have not sought to take it further. I do not think they will be whole until they do find the families of their blood but I cannot do it for them. And I am not kidding myself that it will be easy for me if, or when, they do. The last time I tried to encourage Jessie to search she told me that I talk about adoption too much and to just shut up about it. We cannot talk to Joe much at all these days and he has always acted as though it was too distressing for him to talk about his first mother. Jessie identifies as Aboriginal but Joe doesn't anymore, not outwardly anyway. His resentment runs deep I think, although he does still live with us.

Four years ago our daughter, who is also someone else's daughter, gave birth to a lovely boy. He is the light of my life and my grandson by adoption. His birth and seeing him with his mum has brought me closer to the reality of having your child forcibly taken from you. I dread to think what it would have done to Jessie if that had happened to her. With her son's birth she met, for the first time, someone who looks just like her. She has become more settled and is a good mum, although it was a rocky road at first in a brief marriage and with subsequent battles over access; and with real fear on my part for the possible outcome.

And what of me as an adoptive mother? I know that there are many sad stories of adoptions that have gone wrong for various reasons but I also think that most people do not have a clue how adoptive parents really feel. In October 1998 I heard Deborah Cheetham being interviewed by Margaret Throsby on ABC radio and the things she had to say were a great help to me. In spite of all she had been through as an adopted Aboriginal in a white Baptist family she still had empathy for adoptive parents. I cried through most of the interview and when I rang the ABC to order a copy of the interview I was told they had just had two other adoptive mums crying on the phone. I later joined a support group for adoptive mothers but had to travel to Sydney for it. Surely there must be many others out there who would benefit from a local support group where they can tell their stories without judgement or criticism. It is time for us to come out of the woodwork and help each other. As adoptive parents we are *not* irrelevant and our stories need to be told, whether our kids have met their birth families or not.

So, how do I feel deep down under the scar tissue? I know that terrible things have been done to Aboriginal people and that the forced removal of children was a horrendous act, the effects of which are still being widely felt. I know that in the past both white and black young mothers were forced or coerced into giving away their babies. And I know there were other mothers who freely chose to have their babies adopted, and that none of these babies had any say or choice in their own destiny. I also know that these two children who I love have been with us since they were a few weeks old. They have been a huge part of our lives for 26 years and 23 years. The road we have travelled together has often been rugged, but it has also been rich. Their lives are entwined into our lives and our hearts.

We did the best job we could in raising our children and I became a mother to them; a somewhat haphazard and nervous mother, who made mistakes and who has regrets. But we did not adopt them to cause them pain, or as do-gooders feeling superior to unwed mothers or out of paternalism towards Aboriginal people. We adopted Jessie and Joe because we wanted them, and because we believed they had been willingly given for adoption. And through raising and loving them I have been forced to grow, to grow up. I have sometimes felt that Jessie was sent to me for a reason. But perhaps I am being fanciful.

Present-day adoption has swept away the blanket of secrecy and now encourages and expects contact – letters and photos – and counselling support. This is also a tricky road, I feel. In our day we were virtually left to sink or swim and the secrecy, pretence and lies of the past have caused so much ongoing heartache. I now believe that, if possible, Aboriginal children should be adopted into Aboriginal families. The ongoing anger and grief over black/white adoption is not helping any of us in this country I love. There has to be another way.

Bringing Ethiopia home and into our hearts

Joanne Howitt-Smith

Our family is like so many in today's society. It is complex, messy and exhausting. This said we would have it no other way! My husband and I married nine years ago and with each of us having a son and daughter in their teens it would have seemed madness to most of our friends to begin again. Back then I would have agreed with them.

As our children grew into young adults we began to ponder what we might do with the rest of our lives. I was enjoying completing my psychology degree and Ian was completing his qualifications in conveyancing. Life was looking pretty uncomplicated after steering four children through the teenage years. My husband and I are Christians and what happened next should not have surprised us.

A dream was planted in my husband's heart, one regarding the raising of an African child. Most of us were taken aback but this sudden passion was even more a shocking revelation to him, who likes an orderly life. After all, hadn't we done our bit by getting our biological kids to adulthood? Apparently not. He worried over this dream for several months before approaching me about it, and let me say here and now that it took me several dinners and a few wines to even contemplate those teenage years again! I was secretly delighted though that we were going to extend our family and this option was perfect for us as neither of us was able to have more biological children. In fact adoption was a much more palatable option for our older children than the concept of more half siblings. Their lives were complicated enough.

We began the process the following Monday, putting in our expression of interest and defining our country of choice, Ethiopia. There were many hiccoughs along the way and my husband's age was an issue. Due to age criteria of both the South Australian and Ethiopian governments, we found ourselves with an age range of seven to nine years. This, too, suited our family as we were both past the nappy and teething business and were delighted to take on the challenges of older kids. The prospective adoptive parents' assessment where old emotional 'stuff' is brought out to air and then rehashed is both exhausting and necessary. However it is not something that either of us would want to do too frequently. We jumped over whatever hurdles came our way and answered some tough questions. We opened our financial situation and home to scrutiny. It was all very invasive and many times we longed to be private people again.

If we thought that the assessment phase was hard then we were really unprepared for how desperate and *long* the waiting phase could be. It took two very long years from expression of interest to allocation. Just when it seemed that this dream was never going to happen we would receive a little reminder that God had not forsaken it, nor us. Often I felt quite chastened and could almost hear: 'Be still! I'm working on something over here and you will just have to be patient.' We certainly have learned about patience and persistence through this process.

Then came allocation day with *that* phone call to say we had twin eight-and-a-half-year-old daughters. It felt like finding out we had won the lottery or were pregnant after such a long and difficult wait; a mixture of excitement, shock and anxiety. And the day we met these wonderful girls for the first time was truly an awesome experience. Our Ethiopian final process, for some reason known only to God, went through in four to six weeks instead of the usual four to six months and we were able to travel out to Addis Ababa on 16 December 2002.

Once again things fell into place with flights and accommodation, and we met the girls and took custody two days after arriving. What an amazing day! Neither of us could sleep after arrival and we were both up listening to the calls to prayer at four in the morning. It was not until midday that we were able to pick them up and as we had yet to see a photo of them how were we to recognise them? We shouldn't have worried. They knew who we were from the photos we had sent of home and they came in looking tall, well-fed and gorgeous, their hair braided by the nannies into the most intricate zigzags that we call cornrows. They hugged us to death and we cried. I was very worried as to what I should wear. How would I have liked my new mother to look? I shouldn't have worried. Our girls were tentative but eager to learn and explore the backpacks of books, pencils and girlie bits we had brought from Australia. We gave them a Caramello bear each and they nibbled away, putting up a brave front. Later when we had more language at our disposal we were to find out that they hated chocolate! It took two years for them to like it, but now, well, let's just say that Easter is becoming quite expensive.

Our journey with our girls has been eventful. There was and continues to be much adjustment for all of us. The girls grieved over the loss of their family and friends in Ethiopia, particularly over the death of their mother. The challenge of learning to speak a new language was huge for them and hard for us. There were some days when all of us wondered if this was ever going to work and when it would get better. Then a wonderful breakthrough would occur and we would all be back on track, learning to get along and bond.

At first there were many explanations to be made, both at a cultural and colloquial language level. We realised that we could not assume they understood everything we said, and learned to pare down our instructions for tasks. But our twins had come with enormous life skills. They loved to do things the long way, as our grandmothers used to, like scrubbing floors on their hands and knees. The twins were so good at it that you could have had surgery in the kitchen after they had cleaned it. Daily chores were completed with the efficiency of a much older child and it was awe-inspiring to watch them at work. They gained a lot of self worth from their contribution and it seemed wrong to stop them. It made us aware of just how softly our older children had been raised.

Schooling, too, was important to them. Indeed, the girls found it hard to understand why there was such a long holiday before going to school and were very eager to be in class. They settled well into school and were so proud of their recent achievement of full marks in a spelling test given to the whole year four class. This from children who until 21 months earlier had almost no English.

They are adaptable and intelligent girls who have a high need for achievement and social acceptance. They are identical twins but one of the things that still amazes me is that people still confuse them including their poor basketball coach. They are mischievous, as they encourage this confusion. It took only a little while for us, lying in bed with our eyes closed, to identify which of the twins had come into the room, just by their footfall. Their personalities are so different but they delight in swapping their moods and mannerisms.

We discovered through their stories that their mother was a wonderful mum and indeed a hard act to follow. She died suddenly after a short illness and they miss her terribly. Both my husband and I have lost our mothers and know something of the pain associated with this loss. I almost feel I have met her as their descriptions are so vivid, and we both feel it is important to honour their memories. I often feel that when we are standing watching their sporting achievements and their school plays that she is there, too, beaming with pride. Last Mother's Day we started what we hope will be a little family tradition. The girls asked if they could light a candle for their mother. I smiled and agreed but got out three candles. We lit them and then each said a prayer of thanks for our mothers and the gifts that they had left us with. I know there wasn't a dry eye in the house that morning.

Some people ask adoptive parents: *How can you love someone else's child? Don't you feel differently to your own?* My answer to these questions is: each of our children is unique; each comes with their own personality, skills and abilities (and not so charming bits). Therefore don't we all love our children in different ways and for different reasons? Why should the fact that someone else gave birth to these gorgeous girls under difficult circumstances in a different culture make them any less easy to love and care for? In fact it is a privilege to be given the care of these girls, to finish the job that their wonderful mother was unable to finish. Another 'well-meaning' statement is: *Aren't they lucky girls, you are doing such a wonderful thing for them.* If I hear this one more time I will scream. No! is my emphatic answer. They are a gift to *us*, both as individuals and as a family, teaching us patience (no English and very little Amharic leads to lots of frustration let me tell you) and making us look at ourselves and our priorities with new eyes.

Two gifts from India

Fiona Thorogood

It's around 10 pm on 11 December 2002 when our plane arrives in India. After over five months of waiting since allocation we are in India again. Our second daughter, Ashwini, is most likely tucked up in a cot she is probably sharing with one or two other toddlers less than five hours drive away. At 16 months of age she is too young to realise her life is about to change in the most dramatic way. Everything that she knows as normal is about to be upended. In five days she will have a father, mother and big sister who will at first be strangers to her. At least we have had the benefit of knowing that our family is about to change and accommodate a new member. We have had Ashwini's photograph proudly displayed in our home since July.

It seems strange that our adoption journey is about to come to its conclusion. My husband and I always knew that we wanted children; I had hoped for two daughters. We were married young, I was not quite 20 and Darren 23. After a year or two of marriage we started trying to have a family, unsuccessfully. I had suffered some medical problems in my late teens that might have contributed to our fertility problems and eventually we were referred to the IVF clinic. But I couldn't come to grips with all the hormones I would have to take and the lack of available information on side effects. We decided to take some time out and think about how we should best proceed in achieving our goal of having a family. During this time we watched as our siblings started a family and I would cry my heart out and be angry at what life had dealt us. Was I being punished?

A few years race by and we make enquiries about intercountry adoption. Eventually we are approved to place our file in India. Six months later, in April 1998 on Darren's thirty-fourth birthday, we are allocated our first daughter, Menaka. We are over the moon. Our daughter is 13 months old and appears to be in good health. We wait three weeks for our first glimpse of her when photographs finally arrive. She is the most beautiful child we have ever laid eyes on and she is ours! Five months later we are on a plane to India for our first ever trip out of Australia. We are emotionally exhausted before we even leave. I am not the most patient person at the best of times and the adoption process has left me feeling wrung out. I feel like I haven't slept properly in months.

We arrive in India at three in the morning and at 9.30, after about two hours sleep, Menaka is brought to our hotel on the back of a motorcycle that also carries two grown men and a three-year-old boy, all without helmets! This is a moment I have waited so long for, to hold my daughter for the first time. She is even more beautiful than her photographs had shown and so tiny; at 18 months she wears a size triple zero dress with plenty of room to spare. This is the part that no one has prepared us for, or if they have we have chosen to ignore them. Our daughter is a stranger to us and more importantly we are strangers to her.

Menaka is grieving the loss of the life she knew, and she is frightened of us. She sleeps through most of our first day together. Perhaps this is her only form of defence. When she's awake Menaka is happy to cuddle and attach herself to me but will not tolerate contact with her new father. She follows his every move, sucks her thumb and tries to hide her face behind piles of toys. She is watchful and wary. We think she is coping fine, but then we don't know our child very well yet. She isn't yelling the hotel roof down but it doesn't mean that she is accepting her new situation.

We spend the next few days getting to know our new daughter, and she us. Three days after we land in India it is time to fly to New Delhi to obtain an Australian visa for Menaka. I am now totally exhausted. I also have a good dose of homesickness and this is not making me a happy traveller at all.

Our flight to New Delhi is disastrous. Our plane leaves two

hours late and by the time we are finally boarding the plane Menaka is extremely distressed. I had decided to save her evening bottle for take off and she is now over-tired and hungry. Menaka shows us that she is more than capable of crying very loudly after all. While still waiting for the plane to take off she hits her head on my chin and opens up a cold sore on her lip. Her lip starts to bleed all over my pale yellow shirt, and all the while she continues to holler. A sari-clad flight attendant steps up and demands to know what I am doing to the poor child. I try to explain Menaka's distress and why I am wearing her blood on my top. The attendant gives me a withering look, like I am some kind of child abuser, and returns with a hot flannel, almost throwing it at me as she informs me that the least I can do for the poor child is to clean up her bleeding face. I feel like a poor excuse for a mother who has no right to this beautiful Indian baby. It's my turn to bite my lip and try not to cry. I spend the two-hour flight to New Delhi trying very hard, unsuccessfully, to do just that.

The next day we obtain Menaka's Australian visa and spend the following five days being tourists. It is in Delhi that I realise that although I had thought that love and bonding would be instant with my new daughter, this was naïve. Love is something that grows. The first feelings I had for Menaka were more a connection. This connection was born of anticipation. We had spent nearly two years in the adoption process and before that I had spent many more years imagining what it would be like to be a mother. I know now that what I thought I would feel was more like a sweet dream or something seen in a movie. The reality is that I am a stranger to this child. She has spent the last 18 months being cared for by Indian women in an orphanage. I know by the way that she has been grieving that she was loved. At times in the last few days when I have been watching Menaka I am sure that she has been looking for someone else. Perhaps Menaka feels as I do and is trying to figure out how she feels about me. She is looking to me to provide care and affection. I wonder what I was expecting Menaka to give me. Did I really think that she would just open her arms wholeheartedly to me, a white stranger who sounds and smells and looks unfamiliar? Already we are beginning to relax and enjoy each other's company although we are yet to reach that deep love that we will feel for each other in years to come. Our love will grow, it will just take time.

Finally it is time to go home to the welcoming arms of family and friends. If I had any concerns about Menaka being treated any differently than any other member of my family, those fears are forgotten almost as soon as we get off the plane. Menaka charms her new grandparents, our family and friends. After ten days she is relaxed with us. She now loves her new father as well as me, her mum. She still sucks her thumb, but not out of fear and anxiety, more from habit. We spend the next week at my parents' house, visiting city paediatricians, relaxing and catching up with family. And then we return to our rural home where everyone welcomes our new daughter wholeheartedly.

Life resumes and becomes fuller. Having a child is everything and more than I expected it to be. We become involved in our local adoption support group and I co-found the Indian Family and Friends Group. Whoever would have thought that adoption and socialising with other families with adopted children would take up so much of our time?

Every time I go to an adoption gathering I am reminded how much I would love another child. We have been home from India for three-and-a-half years and we haven't even put in an 'expression of interest' form yet. I had thought we would wait no longer than two years to put in our second application to adopt. I am scared though; scared of the interruption to our life, scared of the probing from social workers and wondering if we measure up. It is the contact with families who are waiting to bring home allocated children that drives us to finally submit our forms and get going again.

Although the process of adoption is no easier the second time around, at least we know what to expect. When each lot of paperwork arrives we fill it out quickly and send it right back. We decide to adopt a child from India again and after seven months our file is allocated and we celebrate the fact that we will be welcoming another daughter into our family. Her name is Ashwini and she is ten months old. It seems that all my dreams are coming true. I will have two daughters! This time we get to share our excitement with Menaka, who is excited about being a big sister. She is also excited about going to India and travelling in an aeroplane.

Four months after our allocation and we are nearing (we hope) our final court date in India. Once the court order is handed down we can think about finalising our travel plans and the challenge of booking plane tickets to India during peak season. The adoption agency staff are being very understanding about our frequent enquiries about departure dates. Our travel agent does a marvellous job of holding what tickets she can get without definite dates. In the end we book and pay for our plane tickets without having all the paperwork in India finalised. Our adoption order is granted two days before we leave Australia for India.

We land in India again and our 16-month-old daughter waits for us. This time I have come to India determined to enjoy every moment. Darren and I cannot wait to see Menaka's reactions to her country of birth. We have done our best to prepare her before we left Australia with books and videos. In the car on the way to our hotel she sits between us in the back seat, taking everything in. She laughs at all the horn blowing and mad traffic, even at 10 pm.

We spend the next five days sightseeing and experiencing all the sights and smells that India has to offer. The time is well spent, giving Menaka a chance to acclimatise to her environment before we meet her new baby sister. Everywhere we go Indians are fascinated and supportive of our family situation. It is not often that they would see Westerners with an Indian child. Menaka gets treated like royalty and is told constantly how lucky she is. This makes me a little uncomfortable at times but we quickly exclaim that we consider ourselves to be lucky having such a beautiful child to call our own.

Finally the day arrives. By 8.15 we are in a car to Ashwini, our daughter. Our trip will take us four hours. Menaka unfortunately wakes with a temperature and sore throat, and spends most of the trip sleeping on the back seat under a blanket. Darren and I get to watch the beautiful scenery. When we arrive at our hotel we are greeted by Australian friends. They have been here for three days and have collected a family of three daughters. Their children are beautiful and obviously already bonded with their new mum and dad.

We settle in to our new hotel and have a short rest – then get a call telling us that a car from the orphanage is waiting downstairs to take us to Ashwini. After arriving and spending some time chatting with the trustee of the orphanage our daughter is brought to us. She is beautiful, even if she is yelling her lungs out. I remember Menaka's fear when we first met her and I don't try to take Ashwini from the arms of her *ayah* until she has had time to get used to our company. Finally the moment arrives when I hold my daughter for the first time. Ashwini cries for about 30 seconds then settles in my arms with the help of a biscuit bribe. Menaka is excited to meet her new sister and Ashwini is fascinated by Menaka. After spending a couple of hours at the orphanage getting to know Ashwini and finding out her daily routine and diet from her *ayah* we are on our way back to our hotel. I cannot wait to be alone with our new daughter. Though the staff at the orphanage are very helpful and friendly I still feel intimidated as they watch us bond with our daughter.

We spend the next five days awaiting Ashwini's Indian passport. During our time here we have our handing over ceremony. This is a wonderful occasion that the orphanage organises for us and the two other Australian families also here to adopt. We are greeted, given floral garlands and marked with a *tilak* on our forehead. The orphanage trustee hands us our daughter, even though we have had Ashwini for two days. Darren also has to crack a coconut on a rock, signifying a new beginning. Although there is the usual Indian chaos during the ceremony it is a special time for us as a family and a time we will never forget. It is also the last time Ashwini will see the home where she has spent the first 16 months of her life and the *ayahs* who have cared for and nurtured her. How hard it must be for the people who work in these orphanages. To love and care for a child for such a long time and then to hand them over knowing that they will never see them again. I am grateful to them for their work. Ashwini is a healthy, happy child. She has obviously been well cared for and well loved.

We spend three weeks in India. We even manage to travel with two children, an achievement of which I am very proud. We want Menaka to have time to experience as much of Indian culture as we can before we return home to Australia. I know we will eventually take both children back to India for a holiday, but for now we must make the most of our time.

On New Year's Eve 2002 we are greeted in Adelaide by family and friends. We are a little more tired, dirty and smellier than when we left three weeks ago but we come home with the best gift anyone can receive: family. And finally I feel our family is complete. India has given us two beautiful and priceless gifts to treasure forever: our two daughters Menaka and Ashwini.

Choices (Part 2)

Emma Caldwell

The wait to become parents through local adoption is agonising. There's no preparation, no time frame, only hope followed closely by disappointment. You aren't able to decorate a room or buy things for your baby; there may not be one. You can't plan your life; it may change in just a few moments. You have a goal and no control over the plan of action needed to achieve it. You may have been accepted into the program and deemed suitable people for parenthood but your destiny then rests on the whim of a birth parent who may choose you or not, based on some small prejudice or preference. You aren't selected because you are the most suitable. You aren't selected because you're the next on the list. You are chosen because someone likes your profile, something about you connects with them, calls to them. A photograph and a few clinical details of your life are what your greatest dream rests upon. There is, rightly, no personal appeal, no expression of what you could bring to a child's life, no opportunity to make a connection with the people who, unwittingly, hold your hearts in their hands.

I don't know all the reasons we were chosen to be parents to our children. All I am sure of is that our daughter's birth parents chose us, in part, because they felt we could sympathise with their loss. Having experienced the death of our birth children they felt we would understand some of the emotions they were feeling. Both our children's birth parents chose to relinquish because they wanted more for the child they gave life to. Our son's birth mother wanted a sibling for her son. They all wanted their children to be loved, as they loved them, and to have what they could not give: two parents, married and stable in their relationship, and opportunities for their child they believed they were unable to provide at that time. There is a perception in society that a child is relinquished because a pregnant young girl doesn't want the burden, or doesn't love her child. This is far from the truth. It is sad that people can be ignorant of the depth of feeling you need to make such a drastic and life-altering choice. Relinquishment is chosen with love and maturity and I hold my children's birth parents in the highest esteem because they placed their child's needs before their own.

The time between the phone call announcing our selection and meeting our daughter took forever to pass. It was a blur of meeting social workers, organising furniture and clothing, deciding how and when to tell our families. One of the most frustrating things about this time was that after *the* phone call we could not simply say yes and bring our baby home. We had to attend an interview in Melbourne during which we would get information about our proposed child and her birth parents, their reasons for seeking adoption for their child, and what they were looking for from us. After this meeting Anthony and I were both saying yes but our social worker told us to go away and think about it. What was there to think about? Why would we even contemplate saying no when we were being offered our dream all wrapped up in a pink bunny rug?

One very long weekend later we were finally able to call our social worker and say exactly the same thing we'd said three days earlier. Yes! I advised my employer I was leaving and Anthony arranged time off so we could go to Melbourne for the handover of our daughter. Finally the day arrived and we met our precious daughter for the first time. Sixty centimetres and five kilos and yet she induced such fear and trepidation in me. I was so scared she would scream at her first sight of me and I was petrified that I'd take one look and dislike her. I was almost too nervous to approach her but one look and we were both totally besotted.

We spent our first day with our daughter quietly at her foster mother's home, learning her routine and allowing her to feel comfortable with us. We also found her new name. Anthony sat down with her in his arms and spoke all his favourite names to her. When she smiled twice at Alise he knew that was the right name for her. When Anthony asked me what I thought of the name I agreed it felt right for her. Our second day was spent taking Alise to meet my parents. My father was undergoing treatment for cancer and would not have been well enough to visit us so we turned up on their doorstep with our surprise. As we only had a couple of days in Melbourne and a large number of family members we decided that we would tell them about Alise after we went home so we weren't obliged to visit them all in one day. Swearing to secrecy those few people who knew about Alise we headed home and announced our new daughter with a photograph posted to each of our siblings. Despite our fears, Alise settled in happily and became part of our family with ease. That day was just over six years ago now. Alise is beautiful, intelligent, likeable and eager to learn. She has an inquiring mind that astounds and a depth of understanding that amazes.

Along this journey we have come to terms with some aspects of adoption that frightened us. The most notable was the ongoing contact between our child and her birth parents. This was fraught with danger for us and it was with great hesitation that we agreed to the condition. Our child's welfare was paramount and I could foresee the perils of another woman telling Alise to call her mummy, people arranging to see our child and not turning up. People trying to turn our child away from us or take her back.

I have had to eat my words, so to speak. Our experience with Alise's birth parents has been incredible. We first met them the morning we were to bring Alise home – at their request. It was a nervous beginning; we were all unsure of what to say, how to conduct ourselves. Slowly we all realised that we were in this together, they were no threat to us and vice versa. Alise's birth parents were comfortable with the choices they had made and wanted nothing more than the opportunity to be friends with us and our daughter. They were very clear about whose daughter this child was and they have never wavered from this.

Alise's birth parents are absolutely fabulous people and to my surprise I have been awed by their strength of character. During the process of applying to adopt I had felt a level of disbelief that someone would choose to relinquish their child for truly altruistic reasons. Alise's birth parents have shamed me with the level of maturity they showed in choosing and continuing this course of action. I'm certain they both have sadness for the choices they had to make but we have not seen regret. They are involved in Alise's life on an ongoing basis, as are Alise's birth father's parents and siblings and her birth mother's mother. We have been welcomed into their lives with honesty and love and they have chosen to become part of Alise's life rather than observers. We spend time with them in their homes and they have been welcomed into our home. Our daughter has a larger extended family than many but it's a joy to see her spend time with her birth families and an honour to be included in their lives.

Since Alise came into our lives we have been less frequently targeted by the well-intentioned but intrusive questions regarding children. We still get 'are you going to have another one?' but the majority of people here know that Alise joined us through adoption and if they ask it will be regarding our second application. There have been occasions where I've been tempted to put people in their place, most often with regard to the comments about having a child the 'easy' way. I don't think anyone who knows where Anthony and I have been would classify our path as easy but it's certainly been worthwhile and fulfilling: we have Alise. I have discarded a couple of former friends along the way, people who were overtly offensive about those who would choose to relinquish their child or people who couldn't cope with the idea of us loving a child to whom we have no biological link, and couldn't grasp that there is no difference when you choose for there to be none. I love Jeremy and my other sons no more, no less and no differently to the way I love Alise. They are all my children and they have all left footprints on my heart.

Alise has been brought up knowing how she became our child, aware that she was born to another woman and the reasons she wasn't raised by her birth parents. She has remarkable insight into her situation. She has independently decided she has four parents, all of whom are very special because of the choices they made which enable her to have the life she has now. One of my favourite moments occurred when Alise was barely six and an acquaintance of Alise's birth uncle asked how Alise knew him. With no prompting (and no prior discussion of a similar scenario) Alise replied, 'He's one of my special friends, and that's all I can say right now.'

Alise feels the need to know where everyone fits in her life and yet she has an awareness that casual acquaintances don't need this information. She loves all the members of her birth family she has met, loves all her cousins from Anthony's and my families and wishes for a sister or brother to share her life. Connections are very important but Alise loves for the person not the familial relationship. She knows about our sons and often expresses her sadness for us, and herself; in her own words, she misses her brothers.

Therein lay my only regret: Alise had no sibling to share her life with. I chose to have my tubes tied to avoid further miscarriages and we decided to commit all our resources to adopting a second child. Our second application had been accepted nearly three years before and we felt that perhaps we were at an age when we should seriously reconsider it. I had started to accept that it was unlikely we would be parents to another child, and was at peace because I felt Alise filled our life. We had decided we would give our second application a couple more months and then withdraw from the program if we had not been selected by a birth family.

Within a few days of that decision, to our great surprise, we received a phone call to tell us that we had been chosen to become parents of a little boy. We had almost accepted we were a one-child family so the feelings evoked this time were vastly different. I felt I was in a dream from which someone would wake me and I would discover there was no second child for us. The next three weeks were such a whirlwind of activity I felt dizzy. We had to go to Melbourne for the information session, change bedrooms around within our home (Alise felt that as the oldest she should have the biggest room), find all the nursery furniture and ensure it was still useable, track down clothes to suit and fit a baby boy of some seven months, and move and store about three tonnes of other collected junk.

During these preparations we had to sort out the details of meeting our new son and ensure that Alise felt she was a part of it all. Even though it was only three weeks from the first phone call until we brought our son home it felt like there was a conspiracy to delay our meeting him. One of the unavoidable delays was that our agency was employing new staff and until they had a worker in place, with a valid police check, we could not even meet our new son. Alise was desperate to meet her little brother and wanted just to go and get him.

We got the dates from our agency and the name of our new social worker. Finally, in early March, we were able to meet Michael and begin the process of making him a part of our family. At our first meeting, cradled happily by his foster carer, Michael watched Anthony and me carefully for a while. After a short time the carer sat him next to her and he promptly wriggled and rolled his way over to nestle firmly against my side and gaze up at me, chatting all the while. Once he'd become bored with all the attention from the various adults present he called for a bottle and fell asleep in my arms.

In the month since, Michael hasn't looked back. He has settled into our family incredibly well. Anthony walks into his room in the morning and his little face lights up, Alise follows and it's up another 100 watts, and then me – well I'm mum and we know what that means. Life is hectic, I barely have two seconds to collect my thoughts let alone time to myself. But it's wonderful to watch Alise sit with her little brother and help give him his bottle or listen to the giggles that she can so easily entice from him. Our life is replete with joy in a way it never was before, even though Alise would have been enough if she were the only child we raised. Alise has accepted Michael into her heart as easily as we have, her birth families have as well. In their hearts they see Michael as they do Alise; she's their granddaughter and he is her brother, so he is their grandson.

So we are back to the hard stuff. Getting to know and love another birth family and dealing with all the rigmarole that goes with an adoption placement. Getting permission to travel, permission to immunise, permission to do almost anything, 12 months of being checked by social workers, having our home checked and rechecked to ensure Michael's safety. Completing forms and writing letters. Every last minute of time, every last shred of effort is worth it. It means that Michael is part of our family and we are complete.

The well-came cake

Charmaine Cooper

Suddenly the emptiness disappeared. There had been years of grief. I had lost a baby, my wonderful grandmother and my mother many years earlier. And there was the pain of coping with a lack of identity throughout many years of traumatic IVF. And all the time, we struggled to keep our marriage together.

Tears welled in my eyes but there was no time to let them flow. I had a purpose and a responsibility now. Ian and I had been given the greatest gift of all, straight from the heart of Ethiopia itself, from two very special people we would never know. Our responsibility was to them and our absolute love was for those two nervous children coming through the door towards us.

Mehirat was four-and-a-half when she first fell into our arms and Dejene was two-and-a-half. His big brown eyes followed us with suspicion. We faced many trials while learning to become a family. Mehirat and I battled to see who was going to become the mother of the family and Dejene terrorised us with his hitting, screaming, running away and famous tantrums (quite the talk of the town). Intertwined with these challenges were love and joy. After six months Ian and I appeared to be getting the hang of parenting and our lives together seemed complete.

Our lives could have continued as any biologically connected family but there was an underlying feeling of incompleteness in all of us. Ian and I were frustrated that we hadn't spent enough time in Ethiopia to truly feel we knew the birth country of our children. Dejene was continually asking questions of Mehirat about their time there. And we knew that Mehirat was struggling at times to cope with all that had happened to her.

It hurt us immensely when Mehirat spontaneously burst into tears and could not be consoled. We shared her pain but were at a loss to know how to deal with it. Gradually she began to open up about what was hurting her. In the early days, as her English improved, she told us stories of life in Ethiopia with her Ethiopian parents, vivid stories of her daily activities. But as time went on it became clear that the grief for her birth mother was too much. It reminded me of my own struggle and I would just hold her and cry too.

We decided that we needed to return to our children's birth country. We had remained in contact with Captain Belete, a friend of the children's family. He had assisted in carrying out their mother's wish of arranging adoption for the children. We were indebted to him and had previously promised that one day we would return with the children. We had planned to do this when Mehirat was perhaps 12 years old. To everyone's excitement, however, we touched down in Ethiopia only two-and-a-half years after we first left.

We were all nervous. We knew the trip had risks and we didn't know what we would find or how the kids would react. Although we had travelled many times to developing countries, we were parents this time and it seemed different. We didn't realise at the time that our family at home was frightened that the children wouldn't want to come back. This thought hadn't even entered out heads.

The children had packed their own backpacks and were determined to carry them – sleeping bags included. They had counted down the days before we left. Dejene had lost a night somewhere and said, 'One more sleep before we go.' We replied, 'No, it's today!' The screams of excitement from the kids were tremendous.

The flight was long and we had an eight-hour wait at Nairobi airport. The kids fell asleep as we boarded our last flight back to their homeland. We finally saw the lights of Addis Ababa, the capital of Ethiopia, after a marathon 40-hour journey. We began to relive all the sights, smells and sounds of this country that has become so much a part of us.

After a good sleep and a day delivering money to charities

around Addis, we relaxed that evening with a family from Adelaide collecting their gorgeous second son. I had kept a close eye on Mehirat and noticed she was unusually quiet. She got quite upset if she didn't think Ian was looking after Dejene well enough and immediately took on the role of protector and carer of Dejene again. I was unsure of how she was feeling and exactly what is was that she was reacting to. Although we had seen it many times before, the poverty still shocked us. But Mehirat was seeing it for the first time, despite previously living it. Was she reflecting on her past life, or grieving? Or was she trying to comprehend whether this Ethiopia was the same one that she thought she remembered so clearly? As for Dejene, well, he walked confidently around and just took it all in.

The next morning we were returning to our hotel after visiting another charity organisation when I mentioned that we must contact Captain Belete. Imagine our joy when Mehirat casually said, 'Oh there he is.' And, despite a denial by me, she was right.

We hugged and cried. Belete couldn't take his eyes off the children. He hugged them and told us how bright they were and how much they were like their birth parents. He told us stories about the children and hugged them some more.

He left several hours later although he was very uneasy about doing so. It was as if he thought we might leave again. Although his English had improved we still checked and double-checked the time he was coming to pick us up the next day.

We could not have imagined the day that was to unfold. As he promised, Belete arrived with his friend in a car whose clutch, amongst other things, had seen better days. His friend was to be not only chauffeur but interpreter. We all piled in and watched as the familiar activities of the city traded places with open-air markets and herded animals. With each moment I felt a little more anxious and so did the children. Mehirat was being extra clingy and eventually their nerves gave way to sheer exhaustion as they fell asleep.

We dodged the last few pot-holes before arriving at the township of the children's birth. We woke the children. Dejene was ready for adventure but I could see in Mehirat's eyes this place held far too many memories. What were we doing? Why were we putting her through this? Maybe we should forget all about it and leave on the very next plane.

Belete's excitement was obvious. He pointed out where the children played and where Mehirat went to the shops and his house. Dejene bounded out like he was home, despite no recollections, and continued to behave this way throughout the day.

Mehirat clung to me. As we were about to head through the gate to Belete's house she grabbed my arm and began screaming and pulling me back. I suppose I might have expected something like this but it still caught me unaware. I just picked her up and held her close and carried her screaming and crying into Belete's yard. I certainly wasn't prepared for what happened next.

As we came around the corner, we were greeted by 50 or more people cheering, clapping and chanting. Belete's wife and children greeted us with flowers and kisses and tears flowed from the eyes of the many women draped in their traditional white garments. We were totally overwhelmed with emotion and appreciation for the sincere love these people had for the children.

The kissing had only just begun. Dejene's face was permanently pointing to the sky as he received a kiss on one cheek followed by more on the other side. We were proud of him as I knew he probably wasn't enjoying all this attention. We were ushered inside while everyone was trying to steal a kiss from Mehirat. She just held on tighter and tucked her head into my chest. Tears continued to run down her fine little cheeks.

It was beautiful inside Belete's house. The floor was decorated with grass and incense was burning, as was customary for a special occasion. Many people had brought traditional food and home-made wines to share with us. In the middle was a very Western sponge cake decorated with cream and inscribed with 'Well-came' on top. We felt very honoured.

The afternoon was spent eating, hugging, kissing and crying. We couldn't thank each other enough. We thanked everyone for caring for the children and told them how important it was for us to maintain links with their birth culture and country. We were continually thanked for bringing the children back to them. They were eager to tell us amazing stories about the children and their family and how they had been a part of the family's life. We met godparents, best friends, neighbours and most importantly some of Mehirat and Dejene's beautiful cousins.

It was obvious that the community held Mehirat in high esteem for her determination, kindness and nurturing skills, but mostly her maturity, her ability to handle the tragic situation she had found herself in. I knew Mehirat was a special little girl but had no idea of the responsibility she had had when three to four years of age. It was no wonder she was in so much pain now.

Belete announced it was time to see Mehirat and Dejene's house. We were so excited. The entourage left Belete's home and walked down the muddy roads past straw-laden donkeys, free-ranging chickens and lashed wooden fences. We felt like the Pied Piper with almost the entire community following us. Little boys jostled for Dejene's hand and the women and Mehirat's cousins attempted to console her.

We arrived at a beautiful mud hut. The community had rebuilt the family home from its state of disrepair. It had two rooms and a wooden window. The roof had been given a corrugated-iron veranda. It was a long way from what we were used to, but the love that went into building it made it like a palace to us. How could we ever thank them enough.

As the rains were coming we returned to Belete's home. Gradually many of our new friends began to leave and I watched as Mehirat grew in confidence. It was time to hand out gifts and begin the traditional coffee ceremony. Suddenly Mehirat's tears disappeared. She quietly and quickly slipped into the role of carer and caterer and her smile grew with every gift and coffee she distributed. Then through the door came a stunning-looking girl, just a bit older than Mehirat, carrying her baby sister on her back. She had been Mehirat's closest friend. Initially Mehirat didn't recognise her but memories of their time together were rekindled and for the remainder of the day these girls sat smiling with their arms around each other. Our adorable Mehirat was beginning to return.

The day was drawing to a close and after more tearful farewells we were returned to our hotel. We were physically and emotionally exhausted. We could have left Ethiopia the next day satisfied but we still had four weeks of travelling around this incredible country.

Dejene had been an absolute champion. This country was so much a part of him that nothing had bothered, worried or surprised him. The difference now was that he could tell others about his birth country without having to ask Mehirat first. Wherever we went he seemed to find some little boy to play with and attempt to teach him to kick with an Aussie Rules football. He was happy, relaxed and ready to take on any adventure, be it on mules, climbing mountains, visiting rock-hewn churches, or tucking into another spicy meal of *injera* and *wot*.

Each day we watched Mehirat walk a little taller and relax a bit more. We watched her slip into her beautiful Ethiopian gait and carry herself with such pride. We loved it when she decided to wear her delicate Ethiopian shawl around her head and shoulders like all the Ethiopian women, and demand Ethiopian food at every meal. We laughed at her attempts at remembering the language and cried with her in her compassion for those struggling to survive in the street. She was blossoming.

All too soon our journey was coming to an end. We had seen and done so many exciting things. We were in awe of the generosity and love the Ethiopian people have for each other, but especially for their children – our children. We had spent more time with Belete on our return from visiting the north and have no doubts that he loves Mehirat and Dejene as his own. Saying goodbye to Ethiopia and especially to Belete was difficult but I think each of us knows that we will return again one day. That made it a little easier.

Since arriving home we have been able to reflect on our adventure and decide whether it was the right thing to do. Ian and I feel like we, too, are a part of Ethiopia and the stories and understanding we have acquired about our children can only make us better parents. Dejene has spent many hours talking to his class, family and friends about his holiday and his birth country. His pride in knowing about Ethiopia and being Ethiopian is wonderful to see.

And Mehirat . . . well, we have not had one spontaneous burst of tears since we have been home. While some times for her, especially those first few days in Ethiopia, were extremely hard, it seems that she was able to let her grief out and lay it to rest. Her birth parents are constantly and lovingly talked about now but with a sense of closure.

Would we have done it if we had the choice again? Yes. Yes. Yes. While we know that all stories don't have such happy endings, for us it was certainly the right thing to do. As Mehirat said as we left Belete's house on the day we met the community: 'Mummy, please tell Belete to thank everyone. I know I looked sad but in my heart I was happy and this has been the best day of my life.'

PS Some comments from Mehirat after her return trip to Ethiopia: When I went to Ethiopia I thought it was amazing. I found the houses interesting and seeing all the Ethiopian kids. When I saw my family and community I started crying because I was happy to see them. I guess at the start I was a little bit scared. I liked seeing my godmother and my best friend again. My house looked different. I don't know why, but it did. I told my dad he would hit his head in it and he did. Now my mum and dad know why I don't want to move to Port Lincoln because I used to live in Gojam, which was in the country, and I liked it there. Captain Belete was so nice. I really would like to go back to Ethiopia because it is fun and I could eat *injera*. I love Ethiopia.

Challenge

*I still don't know if I have selfishly meddled
with the blueprint for these children's lives
or whether I was always meant to be a part
of the blueprint.*

From Joy to Grace —
maybe someday

Deb Levett-Olson

Robina, an older Filipina child, came to us as a surprise allocation in difficult circumstances. A week after the allocation, while walking my aged cocker spaniel, Joel, in the parklands I was overcome with a sudden feeling I can best describe as a sense of grace. I felt honoured that we were being entrusted with the life of this seven-year-old. This was followed by an overwhelming surge of joy at the knowledge that I would soon have the daughter I had always wanted.

When I arrived home I told Lee I would like to name our daughter Robina Grace or Robina Joy. He agreed with my choices and in the ensuing discussion we decided to wait until we met Robina to see which name suited her best.

We arrived in Manila in late November and in another surprise it was arranged that we would collect Robina three days earlier than anticipated. That night I slept fitfully and as punishment for my constant bragging about becoming a mother without hours of labour and stretch marks I was stricken with my worst period cramps in years. I awoke to a beautiful Manila morning and, in a friendly little Chinatown shop, the best mug of coffee I have ever enjoyed helped me get moving.

We hailed a taxi to make our way to the orphanage. Radios in the taxis seemed permanently tuned into the American 1970s. Simon and Garfunkel's 'Bridge Over Troubled Water' poured out. Without warning I burst into a flood of tears. Lee was concerned and I found it hard to explain that a bad night's sleep mixed with nervous anticipation was a sure mix for an emotional outpouring. I knew my life was about to change forever. I had no regrets about the decision we had made; after years as a teacher working with seven to eight-year-olds surely I was up to any challenge Robina could dish out. A small part of me feared the unknown but this fear was soon put to one side – or so I believed.

At the orphanage we were shown to the cottage where Robina had spent the last three years. She was the oldest child among six girls and 20 boys. I had steeled myself against sad conditions with the children all crying out to be adopted, but it was quite the opposite. We were greeted by a lively gaggle of kids aged between two and seven years who all had the important job of showing us Robina. There was a mood of celebration in the cottage mixed with loud good cheer and attention seeking. I finally made my way to my new child, gorgeous in her party frock and shoes.

'This is my beautiful Robina.'

'*Bina* not Robina!' I was promptly told by the chorus around me. I sat down close to Robina and attempted to say '*Maganda anak babae, masawerti mama and dad*' ('Beautiful girl child, lucky mama and dad') but it was lost in all the noise, bustle and general excitement. Robina's response was shyness.

After a short time all the children were shooed away by staff and Robina shyly showed us around the cottage. I was relieved that she showed no reluctance about being with us. She held my hand as I imagined she would and sat on my lap while the final paperwork was completed. So far she appeared comfortable with me. Apart from some internal hysteria at the sight of lice waving to me from the top of her shiny black head, things were going well. Her *ochi* told me that Robina had been a favourite and she was sad to lose her. I promised to do my best to be a good parent to Robina and thanked her *ochi* for her years of care.

When we eventually left the orphanage it was with a sense of sadness for loss Robina was sure to feel but relief to be able to start working on a new life together. At our hotel I introduced Robina to a new doll I had chosen for her but she showed little interest. I followed this by sharing a book of Australian animals. It was a struggle to engage her interest and Lee suggested we eat.

We lunched well together and then went shopping. Here my first concerns set in. I now know that Robina had not set foot outside the orphanage in the time she had been there. In our ignorance and excitement at buying her new clothes we took her to a glitzy Western mall all decked out for Christmas. Robina went *berserk* (by my standards). She seemed incapable of walking but rather skipped, ran, hopped, slid and boogied. She swung the possum we had given her around by the tail and if I didn't know better I would say she put in some extra big swings in the china and glassware department. Lee had been changing money and when I finally met up with him I wailed, 'Aagh, she's ADHD!' Lee reassured me this was probably not the case but having taught a number of attention deficit students in the past I was hard to persuade. I won't even begin to describe the impact of chocolate ice cream.

The next day we shifted to Bianca's True Home in the tourist district of Malate. This family-run hotel, in contrast to the typical high-rise, palatial, ritzy hotels in Manila, gathered single-storey units into a small compound surrounding a swimming pool. This place away from the busy crowds of Manila helped preserve my sanity, but it was also the place where the relationship with my much-desired daughter began to fall apart.

Though I have promised Robina I will not write about my first failing as a new mama, a word of advice for new adoptive parents: constantly check if your child needs the toilet.

By the time we arrived at True Home, Lee could see the strain between Robina and me. I had mentioned to him on numerous occasions that she was giving me 'the look'. I work in predominantly female workplaces and Lee and I had often discussed how women interact negatively with each other via looks instead of straight, productive talk. The message I was getting via 'the look' and the way she clung to Lee was: 'He is mine. Get lost!' This made it abundantly clear that Robina had decided to see me not as mother but as rival. This came as a shock as I had ignorantly assumed a little girl would be excited to have a mama but that the dad would need to work for her affection.

Lee reassured me that when she saw he was not going to play this game, she would give up. He suggested I take Robina for a swim in the pool; we were sure she would enjoy that. Robina dressed in her new floral bathers, I grabbed the camera, and we headed to the pool.

I held the camera ready for Robina's first swim in a pool and she enthusiastically entered the water. In seconds she was out of her depth and struggling to keep afloat. I dropped the camera, leapt in fully clothed, and grabbed her. I clung to her, keen to keep her in the pool because I believed if she got out she wouldn't get in again. Robina held me through sheer fear. I looked up to see the owner of the hotel and felt embarrassed. It was not a day that would qualify me for 'Mother of the Year' awards.

It went downhill from there. Robina's rejection became overt and I found it very painful. She refused to hold my hand, preferring to run into traffic and around behind us to hold Lee's hand. When in the pool I would carefully throw a coin near the shallow edge for her to retrieve. She would fling the coin to the furthest, deepest parts of the pool with malicious glee. In restaurants she would put her hand out for the menu and then pull back if I passed it; from Lee she would happily accept it.

Even though I kept up an internal adult dialogue – *you are the adult, you can handle this; remember the loss Robina is facing; she must feel powerless; change can be traumatic* – I still had moments of self-pity. One night in a lovely Indian restaurant I was feeling particularly tired and fed up. In a fit of pique I pulled my chair away from both of them. 'Well done,' murmured Lee quietly, 'you've given her what she wants.'

Lee worked hard making it explicit to Robina that we were all to build a relationship together. In our morning routine, Lee would give me a big hug and one to Robina. It was then our turn to hug each other. Robina clearly didn't want to and I don't find hugging comes very naturally to me, particularly when I'm being rejected. To complete this 'chore' I would play games, like walking towards Robina with my eyes closed, deliberately missing her and hugging the door instead; or turn her upside down, hug her legs and tell her feet 'I love you!' Robina laughed a lot at my jokes and genuinely seemed to enjoy my efforts, but within minutes would find ways to let me know I remained a rival, not her mama.

After e-mailing a sympathetic Australian friend that Robina was the little princess, Lee the handsome prince, and I was relegated to wicked witch of the west, I decided to stop trying so hard and just see to Robina's practical needs. Even trying to ingratiate myself by encouraging her towards a pink, frothy, vomitous party frock I knew she liked brought rejection; she chose instead her dad's favourite, a pretty but more practical lemon dress.

The Philippines is a beautiful country, but I have little recollection of places we visited. I do know that when I stepped back I could recognise a strong, confident daughter with excellent problem-solving skills. This defied my expectations that I would be coaxing a shy, anxious child out of her shell and teaching her to take on life's challenges. Robina took life by the horns. She raced from place to place with a total disregard for spatial issues, prompting constant fear she was going to crash into people or dash out on the road.

My final recollection of Manila was walking through the airport. Robina, holding Lee's hand, bounced along like Daffy Duck on speed. I held his other hand whining about the kid I taught two years previously who acted like *that* until we stuffed Ritalin down his throat to calm him. It amazes me that Lee did not leave both Robina and me sitting in the Manila airport and fly home on his own.

Robina took to the flight with her usual enthusiasm, giving a loud whoop as the plane accelerated on take-off. We decided to take a walk. She showed a predisposition for pushing every button in sight as well as telling people how to do their job, particularly if technology was involved. After our little amble we made a toilet stop. Lee and I were outside the cubicle chatting when I saw a steward frantically stumbling down the narrow aisle with fear on her face. I was mortified when her dash ended outside Robina's cubicle. She banged on the door, yelling 'Who's in there? Open the door!' She asked the group, 'Does anyone know who is in there?' To this day I cannot believe my response. 'No,' I quietly replied and sidled away to my seat. In the meantime Robina opened the door still hoicking up her knickers. The steward explained that Robina had pushed an emergency button and a minor panic followed. Lee apologised and fortunately the hostess seemed relatively forgiving.

In Australia things settled down. I felt more secure being in familiar territory. Lee returned to work while I had leave to help Robina settle in. My daughter quite cheerfully spent the days with me visiting friends and playing crazy games (like throwing mud at each other!), and when I needed a break she happily watched videos. She was always very excited to see her dad come home. The rejection was not so intense but it was still there, particularly when competing for Lee's affection. Each morning Lee would kiss me, then kiss Robina. If he was silly enough to give me another kiss she would line up for her second. If he hugged me for a microsecond longer she would demand an extra microsecond too. Our goodbyes were truly pathetic: we would still be waving long after the car had turned the corner, neither of us wanting to finish first, each of us the more dedicated woman.

At home I was soon more relaxed, recognising that if I had been placed on a pedestal as Lee had, then once the shine rubbed off there was only one direction: down. But being placed lower than an earthworm meant managing to rise to dung beetle status was a triumph. I could see that I would make ground if I could just be patient and be myself.

After Robina had been with us nearly two months and close to her eighth birthday, we were sitting together on a wall at the beach. Lee was in the middle and we had an arm each across his back. Things were actually quiet (unusual for the past few weeks) and I leant back to look at Robina, who had simultaneously done the same thing. I screwed up my nose and poked my tongue out at her. Robina responded in kind. Lee calmly said, 'Cut it out, you two.' But for the first time his interjection was not needed because I knew at that moment a truce had been called. We were at last going to begin developing a relationship not dependent on our connectedness with Lee. At last after many moments of joy we had a moment of grace.

Two days with Robina had been enough to show us that she was too full-on to have much grace and she certainly lacked graciousness. She was, however, full of the joy of life and brought us much joy. Beside the pool at True Home she became Robina Joy. Robina is proud of her name and knows the story behind it.

When she recently asked if she would ever become Robina Grace I tried to keep a straight face as I responded that a change was unlikely. We were happy with the choice we had made.

Robina is now on the cusp of adolescence. She is a confident, compassionate, bright girl with a burgeoning sense of social justice. I sometimes mourn the quick loss of my little girl but I can see the next stage of her life will be interesting, challenging and exciting. I am proud of the positive respectful relationship we have built together and believe this will be a great support to us both during the next few years.

As we embark on this new stage with her we are also beginning another journey. We are beginning the process of adoption again. We believe Robina is ready to be a positive mentor to a younger sister or two. So I hope in the not-too-distant future I will again be strolling through the parklands with my new canine companion, Amber, and her energetic side kick, Jedda, and sense some new names waiting.

Grace would be a lovely gift but I think this time we are prepared for almost anything.

PS A last word from Robina:
I am Robina Joy. When I first met my parents I was filled with joy, so Joy is a good name. However, I felt some sadness at leaving my friend Bernadette. I often wonder if Bernadette has found a family to live with. I am now 13 years old and discovering how tough homework can be. I feel supported, loved, and respected by my parents (and my dogs). Being adopted, and my parents giving me a dog, Jedda, are the best things that have happened to me. In my heart I know I have a bright future and the same for my sisters who are still to come.

Children of paradox

Anthea Hunt

My story of intercountry adoption is flavoured with the uniqueness of circumstance that we are all afforded as individuals. I began this journey as a married woman, having given birth to both a son and a daughter. As a couple we had always considered transracial adoption as a valid and compassionate means of expanding our family. As a young girl I remember wanting a large family of coloured babies; the diversity of humanity has always fascinated me. In the post-adoptive months my marriage broke down and I divorced, so my journey is one of a sole parent. The children's father has had very little contact over the years.

I have five beautiful children: Ellen is Filipina and 23 years of age; Tim (biological son) is 21; Banjobe, also 21, is from Thailand; then comes Elisha (biological daughter), 17; and my Ethiopian foster daughter, Emily, 15. Tim lives with friends, the others are home. The legacies of those formative years spent in orphanages and the pain of abandonment are with me in daily life. The kids grew up and have blossomed, but in essence, much has not changed. Despite endless love, education, opportunity and professional support, my adopted children still show evidence of emotional damage. I struggle with the reality that many windows of opportunity were closed a long time ago and I believe issues of abandonment shouldn't be confused with those of adoption. I am nourished by an intense spiritual life, which in turn nourishes my family.

As a couple we embraced the pre-adoptive process with commitment and vigour, our choice unrestricted regarding the ethnicity, age or sex of our child to be. I had given birth to two healthy and delightful babies, so we felt we could take on an older child with special needs. I believed we were both excited but realistic. The screening and documentation formalities went well and our file was soon in Thailand. Having two young children, Tim and Elisha, certainly helped pass the time, but being an organised person, having to wait was disempowering for me.

Our file was in Thailand for only a short time before the phone call came announcing that we had been allocated a seven-and-half-year-old son. The vacuum cleaner was shoved back into the cupboard, Elisha into her car seat and I was off, driving to the adoption office so I could have our son's photo in time for my husband's return from work. I slept with that photo under my pillow for months.

After about ten months we emerged from a pitch-black night sky over Bangkok into a seemingly endless ocean of lights. I had travelled before but this was more magical, more profound than any other plane descent I'd experienced. Tim and Elisha were exhausted but excited. We slept briefly at the hotel before my husband phoned our social worker.

The following day, in consuming heat and humidity, we drove from the orphanage for the first and last time. Looking back through the taxi's rear window I saw a tide of animated children disappearing into the dust. No one else looked back, but it was a defining moment for me. By this time, the little boy who'd been frozen with fear in the orphanage's office was thawing out. Banjobe was taking cues from Tim and Elisha and playing with his new Ninja Turtle cap. Tucked into my purse was a little black-and-white copy of a photo of Banjobe at one year of age. The staff wouldn't give me the original. This is the only visual reference that we have to my son's existence prior to the age of seven years. To this day he says he was crying in the photo because he 'wanted a mum'.

We enjoyed a family holiday addressing bureaucratic needs and arrived home tired but happy. Banjobe saw more of his country with us than he'd ever seen before and we all share some great memories of this time.

While in Thailand I gathered that Banjobe had great difficulty communicating with fellow Thais. Once home I took him to an Ear, Nose and Throat specialist. Exploratory surgery identified malformations within his ears and a significant hearing loss, either congenital or resulting from damage in utero. The doctor's manner indicated that it didn't really matter in such a child, after all he was lucky to be alive. Banjobe signalled to me that I could cut off his ears as they didn't work anyway!

Despite some sibling rivalry and Banjobe's challenging behaviours, the kids got on well. Banjobe bonded very quickly to both me and Elisha. He was captivated by his little blonde curly-haired sister and she soon became his second mother. Tim and Banjobe developed a fundamentally sound and 'matey' friendship. I was always mindful that Tim also needed his own world, somewhere without his brother.

Prior to travelling, friends had tried hard not to show their discomfort regarding our prospective adoption. Most were pleasant, many questioned our motives but some questioned why we would do this to our 'real' children. A few were rude. When the extent of our son's hearing impairment and 'non-specific neurological disorder' became evident (Banjobe had been diagnosed with severe expressive and receptive language deficits, despite a high IQ) most people distanced themselves out of awkwardness or ignorance. Some were cruel, asking if I 'wished I could return him'. I didn't have cause to see those people again.

Sadly, my husband was also in denial of Banjobe's special needs. He distanced himself from us all. In hindsight I realise he had difficulties with parenting someone else's child *and* a child with special needs.

Despite this our paperwork went in for a second adoption. Things happen as they are meant to. I believe Ellen was meant to find us and I hope, also, some happiness.

Once again while vacuuming – and I don't do it often – the phone rang from the agency regarding a 'special needs' adoption, an eleven-year-old Filipina girl, whose placement with another family had broken down. My husband acquiesced. I was genuinely happy to welcome this new daughter, so Ellen was placed with us.

Ellen had been abandoned by her birth mother on a busy Manila street corner at the age of four years. She was malnourished and could recall nothing except her mother's Christian name. She spent the next seven years in a Catholic orphanage and was placed into her first Australian family at ten years of age. The placement lasted 18 months. I collected Ellen from school and then called by her former home. Her belongings were laid out on the veranda for us to collect. I was told the family never wished to hear of her again.

Soon after this my marriage was over. I had a few friends left but no energy to put into those relationships, so the focus of my life became family. I struggled, without resentment, balancing the needs of children, work and a mortgage like most single parents. Banjobe's needs almost consumed my life. I was ever mindful that in less than three years Tim and Elisha had gained a brother and a sister emotionally younger than both of them, and lost their father to another family. They were times of survival, not clarity, and I was troubled by fatigue and depression.

I cleaned out my life and in some instances I was quite unforgiving. I said goodbye to many friendships, those people who could not include my adoptive children in the same manner as the other two. I no longer shopped where some of my children were treated in an inferior manner. I left the church that refused to baptise my son – a child with a disability – until he'd completed the theory. I stopped attending post-adoption functions. I felt embarrassed that I couldn't relate to 'couple experiences'. I didn't want a partner, but you know, those crazy societal perceptions! I wish I had swallowed my pride and persisted because my children needed those get-togethers more than ever. It was an intensely lonely time but out of it came tremendous spiritual growth and an unshakeable sense of family.

Ellen had to settle in with all of this going on. She had attached to her father and so suffered badly from the fallout. Her manipulative behaviours and cruelty towards Elisha and me created emotional havoc at home. As much as I could understand why she was stealing from us due to her background of neglect, it was draining to manage. After 11 years Ellen will still quiz me when I leave the house. I well understand the reasons why; I know that her mother never returned for her. But it can be suffocating. Now when I leave the house I always inform Ellen of my itinerary and estimated time of arrival home.

From a young age, it was not uncommon for Ellen to disappear for days at a time. She can be extremely jealous of the others and I feel sad that she does not feel more secure. I realise now that she entered my life when my personal and financial resources were at an all-time low. I couldn't be the mother she fantasised about and I think her games were an unconscious punishment for that. I still try to set firm boundaries. Ellen has never initiated any contact with us unless she wants something. This is not because she is unkind, but rather is about her lack of understanding of relationships. It hurts the others; they often feel used, like the hired help. The real girl, when you see below the pain, is warm and witty. Ellen always acknowledges my birthday with lovely cards and gifts, but I feel she has never touched base just to say hello to me.

When the kids were young and cute people responded to them with a sense of novelty. At primary school they were treated with the same sort of dignity afforded to their peers. Being in a special education centre for the hearing impaired saved Banjobe's life. Without the talent and dedication of a handful of teachers I don't think I'd still have my son. They always saw the boy as separate from the issues and they always addressed those issues, as best they could, in a dignified and caring manner. But I had no idea of the journey ahead. As Banjobe matured physically, he was no longer a novelty item. For all of this country's catch-cries of tolerance, equal opportunities and multi-culturalism, my family has experienced racism first-hand.

Banjobe loved and succeeded at football, but it seemed the better he played the more he was targeted with verbal abuse. It got to the stage where I could no longer watch games because of what I heard on the sidelines. He was vilified on more than one occasion and called things like 'a mongrel retard'. It wore him down, until eventually he gave footy away.

When Banjobe was old enough to date it wasn't difficult to

read the minds of some parents. An ex-friend once said to me: 'People don't like to see boat people in SAABs.'

As Banjobe reached the age of wanting to go out alone it became evident that he was being treated with suspicion, scepticism and often hostility. At 13, out with his brother and some friends, Banjobe was forced to the ground and hand-cuffed by four police officers because he was swearing in a public place. As he went about his everyday business shopkeepers, security staff, police and transport personnel would interrogate him. He couldn't spend his generous pocket money without being suspected of stealing; he couldn't wait at a bus stop without police stopping to search him; he was fined for jay-walking; and when he missed a bus and was waiting for another the police moved him along for loitering.

As Banjobe grew older it became increasingly evident that he was having psychotic episodes, usually involving a fear that someone intended to harm him, and at 19 he was diagnosed with schizophrenia. When he left the house it was common for him to phone me, distressed, on his mobile. I still feel sick when our phone rings. I put my 24-hour contact number and relevant details in his wallet. His siblings, especially Elisha, watched out and advocated for him in my absence. More than once I was called to a police station to find marks on my son's skin and vague and dismissive responses from the arresting officers. Banjobe was usually embarrassed, confused and incensed but never unkind about the police; he still looks up to them and is scared of them. He would ask me, 'Mum why they do this, I'm a good boy.' All in all, he was a good boy but given his sensory and language deficits, it was always easier to presume this intelligent, well-built Asian boy was drunk, drugged or had attitude.

Banjobe has a loving girlfriend who understands life. Natalie is Indigenous and has a strong sense of family. Banjobe chooses to leave the house accompanied by Natalie or his family only. He has a brand new car and his learner's licence. Being handed his keys was one of 'those' moments. This young man is a loving son and brother, also a very talented artist but since his onset of schizophrenia, he rarely draws. I hope that changes.

Ellen's encounters with racism are not as vivid but just as painful. She and Banjobe have been abused in public places, told to go home or purposely misled. People constantly make inappropriate remarks of a sexual nature because Ellen is quite beautiful and takes pride in her appearance. Some people have even asked me if she is promiscuous. By contrast Elisha, who is a model, can wear skimpy clothes without attracting the same level of scrutiny.

Ellen won't acknowledge she had a mother prior to me, though I think she remembers her. She has spoken little about orphanage life, though on one occasion she did tell me about being hit with sticks. Her emotional responses indicate past abuse.

Banjobe's language disorder has meant that he could not have processed information in the same manner as his peers. But he has described many of his pre-adoption experiences in detail. He has told me of hunger, boredom and abuse. His peers, starting to perceive a difference, alienated him and he talks, too, of loneliness. True to his nature he shows no anger or resentment about his orphanage life. He chooses to believe his birth mother is dead. This rationale makes sense to him and has allowed him to move forward.

Both Ellen's and Banjobe's full names were retained and we gave them Western second names. I have always considered their birth names to be their only true links with their personal histories, something they bring from their mothers and families of origin. Giving them second names has given them options but they have always used their birth names proudly.

Ellen's skin and teeth demand a lot of care, testament to the years when her mother must have struggled to care for her toddler. She never mentions the Philippines and is often angry and manipulative. But she has achieved a lot and I am extremely proud of her. She is now at TAFE and has a job. Our relationship is evolving into something solid and special.

Tim works long hours but is in regular contact with me and his brother and sisters. He is a kind and gentle young man. I have to continually remind him that the only thing he owes me is his happiness ... and to fix the computer ... and to change the light-bulbs (being the tallest in the family!).

Elisha is expecting a baby early next year. The father is

Indigenous so I'm pretty excited about more brown babies! She has struggled with Banjobe's illness, being so close to him; they have had to redefine their relationship somewhat. Banj is excited about being an uncle.

Emily, my Ethiopian foster daughter, has been with us for over a year now. She was born during the great famine of the 1980s. Emily's biological mother died early in her life, leaving her grandmother and aunty to care for her. Emily was sent to an orphanage and relinquished for adoption as her grandmother aged. Sadly, her placement with an adoptive family broke down when she reached adolescence. Emily ran away, vowing never to return to them. After temporary alternative care Emily entered our family. Some days Emily appears to be meshing and connecting with our family, and then I look at her and think she chooses not to belong to anyone.

Emily was openly confused and challenging regarding her identity and her place in the world. We researched her birth family. She will always be a special girl with lots of lovely qualities but since beginning my story she has left my care. She has chosen to live with her boyfriend and will have nothing to do with us. I have given her an open invitation for lunch but she has declined. I wish her good things.

I grieve intensely for my adoptive children's birth mothers, especially at milestones in the children's lives. I want to let them know that the babies they bore are much loved and valued, that I have been privileged to mother them and to be the caretaker of these 'global citizens'. I have taught myself to do this in meditation, it's the best I can do. I visualise these women far removed from me geographically and culturally but at the very core of my life. In lonely times it helps me immensely. At school graduations and twenty-first birthdays I tell my children how proud their birth mothers would be. Banjobe interrogates me as to how I know and I let him in on the 'secret mother's business'.

I would do little differently if I could turn back the clock, but I would be more trusting of my own intuition and less of professional services. Perhaps I would spend less time being a lawyer, teacher or psychologist and more of just being me, mother and soon to be grandmother.

I value laughter, play and a sense of humour. I still don't know if I have selfishly meddled with the blueprint for these children's lives. I feel shame that our Western world sanctions Third and developing nation debt and that I am an active stake-holder in a scenario that sees young people taken, without their consent, from the land of their birth. Having said that I believe, with absolute resolve, in the United Nations Declaration on the Rights of the Child and the entitlement of family for every child.

The manner in which my children take their place in the world humbles me. Without trivialising their histories I have always expected them to be accountable for their treatment of others and I expect them to count their blessings, for they are many. In turn I live a full and blessed family life; they are affectionate with me and each other. intercountry adoption has given my life depth and a unique window into humanity.

I hope they are happy. They bring me much happiness.

Forever family

Janine Weir

Two beautiful Korean baby boys grew in our hearts and became our sons, the core of our Korean-Australian 'forever family'.

My husband and I naively thought that our friends and family would give us unconditional love and support in our parenting journey. The reality was that none of them really understood transracial adoption. Very few even understood adoption.

It would have been easy to take the idealistic view that love is enough in the parenting of our Korean children: the notion that we are all the same, that race doesn't matter, that love of the family will be enough to see us over any obstacle.

However, working through the paper trail required for international adoption, we soon found that our focus had changed to fulfilling the needs of the child as much as fulfilling our own need to be parents.

When each of the planes departed Seoul with one of our beautiful children, they didn't leave with a Korean child who would suddenly become a white Australian child. Yet that was the way some people expected us to act. Instead, our family would become Korean-Australian. We would embrace many things Korean with the same energy and joy our children felt in responding to Australia. We would endeavour to give them a sense of pride in being both Korean and Australian. We wanted to honour their heritage, language, culture and race.

Our friends and family took a little while to digest this fully. They thought our kids were cute and delightful. They were overjoyed that we had a family at last. One by one they started to understand how seriously we were taking it. They, too, began to embrace the make-up of our family. Many began to see the children as bridges between two cultures and encouraged us in our challenges. By the time our second child was a year old we were overwhelmed by the fact that the majority of our friends had taken the journey with us.

Returning to Korea for our second son, our eldest stunned social workers at the orphanage with his command of Hangul, the Korean native language. The social worker embraced me as though I was a Korean mother and spoke to me in informal Hangul. Our eldest announced to us: 'Mum, I am Korean, you're Australian, me too, but you're not Korean – I am Korean, Mum, but I don't live in Korea. I live in Sydney with you, Mum . . .' He chatted happily to market stall owners in his baby Hangul and to children in the street. On his second visit to his original foster mother he communicated easily with her. That was priceless. All the heartache and challenge we had faced in our attempts to promote Hangul within our family had paid off and we had the foundations for the growth of a healthy Korean-Australian pride.

It proved to be a full-time job managing Korean in our lives. It broadened our view of the world and touched our hearts in a way never imagined before. Our 'forever family' would always be at least 50 per cent Korean, given we currently have two Korean children and intend applying for a third.

Our children's day-to-day world is Sydney, so the English language and all things Aussie are dominant, no matter how much we have mastered Hangul or Korean customs and sports. We are sure our children's cousins and close friends will lead them to football, rugby and, in time, beer and surfing. We just hope their Korean pride will also be a balanced part of who they are. In the end they will do with it what they wish; we can only give them the tools for their adult life.

We were lucky to find schools that were truly multi-cultural; where many parents spoke another language with their children and where diverse religious and cultural backgrounds were respected and special celebrations embraced.

Our life with our children is a never-ending series of lessons. We have hiccoughs along the way to remind us why children need a strong sense of self. We have gained an insight into what our children will experience as they grow up. It gives us an under-standing of subjects that we never really understood till now – for example, racism and discrimination. Transracial adoption is so visible and many people believe it's all right to give their input, welcome or otherwise. Hearing us speak Hangul, one close friend was bold enough to tell us how we should be parenting our children, and that included not using Hangul, especially in front of her because she and her husband didn't like it. She felt our children should just be little Aussies. It never occurred to her that our parenting style was none of her business and her comments racist. Giving our children a second language was seen negatively, yet it was socially acceptable for her children to embrace French or Italian prior to an overseas ski holiday. The great sadness in all of this was that our eldest picked up on it very quickly and asked why this friend didn't like his language. Such moments remind us how delicate a child's self-image can be.

In some cases we had to let go of friendships to protect our children. These losses caused heart-wrenching sadness. But it provided the opportunity to show our children that other people were entitled to their opinions although we didn't always agree with them.

When a child is taken from their country they are also taken from much-loved people and from the sounds and the smells of their own culture and language, and placed in a world where all is different and unfamiliar. We found our first son's native language was the most soothing thing we could use with him. It became our melody and when his first words were in Hangul, picked up from his foster mother in Seoul, our hearts broke at the thought that we could have considered taking his language from him. We resolved to work harder on Hangul. We used it at night before bed, after bad dreams, as we dropped him off to school. Special moments were always in Hangul, and I hope it will always be thus.

Those unfamiliar with our children identified them as Korean or Asian and we realised we had to help our boys value this. We saw their differences as a source of pride, not of shame and confusion. But in time we realised that no matter how much we brought them up as Australians in a multi-cultural society, discrimination still occurred. We could not prevent labelling and stereotyping due to appearance. We could only protect our children from the hurtful comments and beliefs of uneducated people by fostering the boys' pride in their unique identity. However to help us understand, my husband and I felt we, too, had to immerse ourselves regularly in activities where *we* were the minority race.

The local Korean community showed us amazing support and love. There is, unfortunately, tremendous guilt associated with the intercountry adoption and they were so thrilled to see that our children would not be stripped of their language and culture. Discrimination against unwed mothers was the reason these children had such limited opportunities in their homeland. But even within Australia there were some Koreans who rejected these children as 'illegitimate'. Twice we have come up against this and both times we were speechless and tearful. The last incident saw us rejected by a church-run Korean Saturday school. My eldest understood the hurtful comments made in Hangul and started panicking and dry retching. I would have done anything to have prevented it.

All these incidents have made us determined to ensure our children have strong suits of armour so people's views will not hurt them. They need to hold their heads up with pride in both cultures.

At our children's *doll jant chee* (first birthday celebration), our friends were stunned to watch beautiful Korean girls performing drum dances, a Korean opera student singing a traditional song, and both our boys in their beautiful national costumes. The transmission of the beauty of their culture was not lost on those who attended. Our children have everything to be proud of, in being themselves: Korean-Australians. We are proud to assist them in this lifetime challenge.

PS An update since this story was written, the arrival of our third child Yoo Jung:
Yoo Jung rejected 'Lily', the name given her by her previous adoptive family and, in baby language, she called herself 'Yoojay'.

We were shocked as she was not yet two years old and had been called both Yoo Jung and Lily for almost equal amounts of time. But we accepted she needed a fresh start and going back to her Korean name altered her body language and removed a lot of her initial anger. She is now forever Yoo Jung as her birth mother intended.

Family day

Peta Brindusa

On 31 May 2003 James and I will have been together for three years. Where does the time go? Though in some ways it feels like we have been together forever! It's an amazing and inexplicable feeling.

I adopted James from Romania when he was just two-and-a-half years old. I was the first single woman to adopt in Western Australia. While I thought getting through the approval process would be a challenge, actually waiting for allocation was more difficult. Eventually it all happened and James and I were together as a family. From the first minute it was an extremely happy family and continues to be to this day.

For me, being a single parent is wonderful. I would like the 'perfect' family which would include at least one sibling for my son, but I think we do very well on our own. James is thriving. The best part about being a single parent is I can have him all the time. Another good thing is that my rules are *the* rules. We never argue about the rules, because he knows there is no leniency. He cannot go to Dad for relief. He can, however, negotiate his way out of a war zone better than presidents of large countries.

The negative aspects of being a single parent are the obvious ones. Of course I would rather be married to someone earning a high wage so I could stay home and not have to work! Instead, I have a part-time job that allows me to drop James at school and pick him up every day. But when school holidays come I want to be with him and I hate going to work. Then I think of my friends and family and realise that these days there are not many women who can stay home even if they are married.

As a single mother with a son I ensure that James has male role models. He spends a lot of time with male friends playing football, cricket, hammering a nail or digging in the garden. These are things he loves to do with them or with me. As a single woman, I need to do these things anyway. He is already showing signs of becoming the 'man' of the house. After watching a Fred Astaire and Ginger Rogers movie he now wants to 'hold me like a man' when we dance. He thinks it's wonderful.

We celebrated our Family Day on 31 May this year with family and friends at our local park. We had presents, party food, a big number three candle on the cake with a kangaroo holding the Romanian flag. The thing we had most of all though, was a strong sense of belonging, fun and laughter (and that was before the wine flowed). We had thoughts of gratitude to his birth mother for doing what she thought would be the right thing.

It has certainly turned out to be wonderful for James and me.

Our adoption journey

Susan Lomman

My international adoption journey was long and tortuous, lasting four years and taking me across two states. In two days it will be the second anniversary of what we call our 'Family Day', the day my daughter Ashleigh and I became a family. The last two years have had their ups and downs but my life is so much richer. I couldn't imagine life without her. I just love being Ashleigh's mum.

I decided by the age of 34 that I probably wouldn't find 'Mr Right'. However, the desire to have my own child was strong and adoption seemed a natural and moral choice. Natural because I was domestically adopted at birth and have always been happy and secure with this knowledge.

At this time I was a resident in South Australia and after enquiries with the agency there I was warned that as a single applicant my chances of success were slim or nil. Perhaps it was naivety on my part or just a huge desire to become a mother, but I continued with my quest. My first paperwork was submitted on 24 October 1998. I went to a series of education nights, six couples and me. I was number 13 – was that significant? The more I heard the more I was sure it was for me. More paperwork. My social worker encouraged me to consider fostering, she knew my dream was almost impossible. I had hours – and I mean hours – of interviews and felt emotionally drained but still determined to keep trying. The social worker felt I was not prepared enough for motherhood and suggested I read more books! I believe I learnt nothing from the five or six books I diligently read. Nothing surpasses listening to other young mums, and young adoptive mums.

I nervously told my mum and dad of my plans. They were in their sixties and we belong to a conservative church. I thought the whole single mum thing might be too much for my parents. As was often the case I underestimated them. I can see them now sitting on my lounge crying, and not with grief. We have always had a special bond because of my adoption and they knew exactly why I wished to do this. My sister and her husband were initially reserved in their support; they had teenagers and wondered why anyone would want children! This surprised me somewhat. They did not have trouble conceiving and I suppose never felt that desperate longing for a child. My brother was very emotional when I told him of my plans and understood my need perfectly.

Months passed. The files of my education group went overseas, mine was still chugging through bureaucracy. Eventually in February 2000 I received a somewhat grudging approval letter from the state Family Services Department. The first paragraph said that I had been approved as a 'prospective adoptive parent' and then the next two pages covered the reasons why under state legislation I would never be allocated a child! Let me point out at this stage that the legislation allows singles to apply, obviously be approved and able to be allocated special needs children. I pointed this out and was told that all children were offered to couples first and 'let's face it, there are no shortage of couples, you will never get one'.

Down, but not out, I wrote to the Premier questioning the process and the legislation. The response just quoted the legislation again. The desire was still there but the energy was waning. After some thought and discussions with others I decided to move interstate and transfer my file. This decision was extremely difficult. My mother was in the end stages of a fight with leukaemia and I had a good job, training position, lovely house and beautiful diabetic cat that couldn't be shifted interstate. It was only with the blessing of both my mum and dad that I made the move.

I applied and was accepted for a position in the capital, rented out my house, packed my things, shifted cat and syringes to my parents, packed my car to the roof and off I went. Family friends allowed me to stay while I looked for accommodation. I soon settled in to my unit and work. My church in Adelaide has a number of churches in other states so my support group was again established. In fact, some of the church members had been family friends for 20 to 25 years.

It was my impression that my file, already prepared to go to China, would simply be transferred, updated and sent. In fact it was 11 months until it left the country.

Once again, interviews, another medical, police checks. My approval in another state meant nothing. I had to do the whole process again, minus the education nights. Paperwork, paperwork again. More delays. Then yet another medical, this time tailored just for China. My doctor thought it was all a bit of a joke by now. My social worker eventually did her report in January 2001 and made quite a deal about the possible scenario of my daughter not accepting my faith and being rejected by the church. This was totally devastating and couldn't have been further from how our church works. I wrote a heartfelt letter of rebuttal to the senior social worker, citing that at no stage had I inferred this may be the case, or had any members of my church been contacted. My concerns were accepted and my home study report rewritten. I felt I had won a major victory.

On the domestic front my mother's condition deteriorated, then improved. She clung to life in the hope that she would see her next grandchild. We all knew that this would not happen but we all need hope. My work was supportive and allowed me a nine day fortnight for many months. I would take the train overnight on Fridays to Adelaide, spend the weekend with Mum and Dad at home, or at the hospital depending on Mum's condition, and then bus back on Monday night. I would arrive early Tuesday morning, go straight home, shower and go to work. This fort-nightly ritual enabled me to have some treasured last months with Mum, catch up with friends, support my parents and spend time with my beloved cat.

Mum passed away on 14 May 2001. This was two weeks after defiantly making it to her seventieth birthday. We were by her bedside at the end. I had dashed over three days earlier. This was the end of an 11-year struggle. My mother's determination has obviously rubbed off on me and she will always be my inspiration in life. For many months after her death I felt anger that my adoption journey had been so unnecessarily long and that Mum had never seen her grandchild. To add to my grief, only six weeks later my cat died too.

The grief was alleviated somewhat by the fact that finally my file left the country for China in June 2001. It had been completed and waiting for a 'batch' to gather since February 2001. Adoption teaches you patience. So I was 'expecting', along with the other three of my batch. During this time I continued to visit Adelaide to support Dad. I worked as many Saturday morning shifts as I could and all through my holidays to save some much-needed dollars. Renting interstate and travelling to Adelaide had dented the back balance.

My thirty-seventh birthday went past and still no child, but at least I was 'expectantly waiting'. I continued to collect things, haunt children and baby shops, and dream.

On 6 April 2002 *the* call came at 6.40 pm. My social worker told me I had a little girl, her birth date and her Chinese name. Just the bare details – but enough. *Finally.* I hung up the phone, put my head down on the table and just howled. All the waiting, difficult interviews, shifting, anger, frustration, and loss of loved ones overwhelmed me. Then joy and numbness followed. I made a rather tearful phone call to Dad. I told him he was now a 'Chinese grandpa'. Choking sounds replied.

The next day my workmates were almost hysterical. Over the months they had hugged, encouraged, passed me tissues and felt very close to my 'expectant waiting'. I received flowers and a baby girl balloon. That night my social worker came around with more details and two photos. Ashleigh looked so serious and I longed to put a smile on her face. More paperwork signing and then phone calls to fellow batch members. The Internet group to which I belong (linking prospective adoptive and adoptive families of Chinese children) was a huge support, both practically (advice, information on medical centres in China, phrase books, hotels) and emotionally. They shared my joy.

The wait from allocation to handover was 14 weeks, an unusually long time due to public holidays in China. This time didn't really bother me. I was a mum and, after such a difficult journey, it was only a matter of time.

On 10 October 2002 Dad and I flew out of Melbourne via Singapore for southern China. We arrived very tired at our hotel late on 11 October, my thirty-eighth birthday. What a present! The next day we met the rest of our batch. Joy, our guide, was patient with the nervous parents-to-be. We were helped to fill out more forms and shown where we could buy baby stuff. We were expecting to meet our babies Sunday evening but that had been changed to Monday morning. Sunday night I packed my baby bag again just to make sure all was there and I re-re-re-checked all my paperwork and lay out my best clothes for an early start the next day.

Surprisingly I slept fairly well and was up at the crack of dawn. I felt it was important to look the best I could on such a special day. Breakfast for our group was almost silent. Everyone was feeling the tension, nerves were stretched. We were supposed to leave at 8 am but the Swedish group before us was delayed and therefore, so were we. By 8.30 we were on the bus. I felt the whole thing was surreal; most people go to a hospital for a baby, I get on a bus in the middle of China! Also I felt quite nervous: was I doing the right thing, had the fight just been for the fight's sake, could I do it? We went upstairs into a large, stuffy room with many flags around the sides and no chairs. The Swedish group were just about to welcome their children. There wasn't a dry eye in the Australian camp and it wasn't even our turn. Then they moved out and we heard some speeches from the Chinese adoption services. I don't remember much except one lady said in English that the children would be distressed and 'there will be much weeping and wailing of children'. She proved to be correct of course.

Then a group of children were carried in by their carers who formed a line. I had been worried that I would not recognise Ashleigh; her photo had been taken at least five months before. However she came in clutching the giraffe I had sent her. They read out each child's Chinese name. When Ashleigh was brought forward my feet just seemed to move. I looked at her in the carer's arms and said 'Hello darling' and stroked her gorgeous, serious little face. After about half a minute I put my arms out and she latched on and that was that. By the time I surfaced to reality everyone else had received their children and the room was loud with the 'weeping and wailing of children'.

Except one, mine, absolutely silent and just staring. She was so beautiful and finally mine. Tears flowed. The room was incredibly hot and humid. Each family posed for an official adoption certificate photograph. The children hated it. Our guide, Joy, was busy rounding up stunned and emotional parents and gently guiding us through what we had to do. Shortly after our photo Ashleigh vomited all over me, herself and inside my dress. I have since learnt that when she is scared she vomits. So my first mummy task was to change her and to try and clean myself.

And so begins my life as a mother. I mentioned the ups and downs. We stayed in China for nearly two weeks and arrived back in Australia two days before Ashleigh's first birthday and four years to the day since I put in my first paperwork.

Motherhood is difficult at the best of times and I guess adoptive motherhood probably harder. Despite knowing it would be difficult, I was soon overwhelmed. Ashleigh is a very determined child and we had many little battles. Some things took me by surprise. For example, I would take a shower and she would scream the whole time. This was despite sitting within sight of me on the mat with a pile of toys. Then I realised she had probably never seen a naked adult. Mealtimes were also tricky. She ate everything and this was certainly a blessing. However, when it came my turn to eat there was more screaming. I lost quite a few kilograms eating very small meals.

But sleeping was definitely the worst problem. She was obviously having great difficulties feeling secure. I would try and rock her – no; try and sleep on the bed with her – no; the only thing that worked was the pram. Here she felt enclosed and safe, so I went with the flow. It was nothing for me to be up at two in the morning pacing the cul-de-sac where we lived. She would wake seven to eight times a night and scream, refusing all comfort.

Daytime was not so bad, as long as I walked for about half an hour three times a day. I lost more weight.

After about two weeks I just crumpled and a phone call to Dad saw him zoom over to help. He took over some of the pram-pushing duties while I slept or washed or cleaned. This was great and they became very close. We were required to visit a paediatrician on returning to Australia and once she had heard my story she diagnosed Ashleigh with a sleep-onset disorder. Ashleigh was also becoming more difficult in the daytime with tantrums 15 to 20 times a day. On the paediatrician's recommendation I returned to Adelaide with Dad for some practical help. I was also advised to use sedatives to try and help Ashleigh sleep and learn that it wasn't to be feared. She eventually developed tolerance to the dose and after several weeks I ceased. For several more weeks I continued pushing the pram, driving the car and becoming more and more frustrated and tired. Ash was gorgeous but I felt she could have done better for herself – I felt a failure as a mother.

The crisis came with my infected gums which required draining and high dose antibiotics. The dentist mentioned that I might have to go to hospital. Impossible. By this stage Ashleigh wouldn't even allow Dad to put her to bed. She was taking three hours a night to go to sleep and there was still no progress with the cot. She would lie on top of me and when I thought she was asleep I would roll her off. Invariably she would immediately wake and scream. I tried to get help from many sources: Child Health (the sister told me to give her more cuddles), my doctor, a paediatrician (he told me after six months it would settle down), a parent help-line, hospitals and specialist post-natal facilities (she was over 12 months of age and did not fit their criteria for help).

Finally I heard of a doctor who specialises in child sleep disorders. He was extremely confident his program would work. I felt that it sounded inappropriate for Ashleigh, like being abandoned all over again. However, when I became ill I had no choice. It was awful – but worth it. He said after three nights it would be over and he was right. She screamed hysterically on the first night for an hour and 50 minutes, vomited the second night and only screamed 40 minutes the third night.

Ashleigh is one determined child. For the first week she slept standing up leaning on the rails of her cot and I had to lie her down. The second week she slept sitting up. But peace reigned. Her eating improved dramatically as the doctor predicted, there were only rare tantrums and the gorgeous Ashleigh, who I had only glimpsed, emerged in full force. Her sense of humour appeared and I can honestly say that on the second night of the program I fell in love. It may have taken three months to come but the relief at helping this little girl was immense.

We have not looked back from there. Sleeping remained a slightly touchy subject for the next couple of months but I knew we had won when after one afternoon sleep I heard her singing in the cot and giggling. On peeping around the door I found my girl doing headstands in her cot. The nightmare was over.

As I have mentioned I felt angry and bitter about Mum not being here to see Ashleigh. However, it was not long after the sleeping was sorted out that I thought back to those frustrated days and learnt something. I know that God is in control of my life. In His wisdom He let me have those last special days with Mum, just quietly. Ashleigh is a dynamo and would have been too much for Mum to cope with.

My next quest in the adoption journey is to adopt a sister for Ashleigh. However, I have returned to South Australia and they have not changed their legislation regarding single applicants. (Five other territories/states in Australia allow and allocate children to single applicants.) So here we go again. I am now corresponding with ministers, so far with little success. But I will keep trying for a while. It would be lovely for Ashleigh to have a playmate, but this time it will not eat at me. After all, I have already been blessed more than I ever imagined.

Trust me

Maxine Donald

Infertility was the key to my journey as an adoptive parent. It was the mid 1970s, with limited options for childless couples. There was at least a five-year wait (with no guarantees) for Australian adoption but this was unimportant to us as we had travelled and embraced the 'global village' concept of life.

We took the plunge. We found a local contact point and prepared to become a multi-cultural family. Most of the others contemplating intercountry adoption at that time were adding to, rather than beginning their families. The urgency and emotion of the Vietnam plight had passed and the focus had shifted to children in orphanages in Sri Lanka and Thailand; to be followed by Indonesia where our application finally went late in 1975. Our first allocation came several months later, a baby boy with a correctable physical handicap. Several weeks passed and the allocation was withdrawn. Tragically our baby boy had died, not knowing he had parents waiting.

Our file was transferred to another contact and fate intervened again; other applicants withdrew after allocation and our file was presented for the waiting baby girl. The court process for intercountry adoption in Indonesia was still in its infancy and it took some months before we travelled to bring home our first Indonesian-born daughter, 11-month-old Yenni Astuti — known to us as 'Tuti'.

Two years later, almost to the day, we arrived in Indonesia to meet our second precious daughter, five-week-old Rini Susilowati, weighing just two-and-a-half kilograms and 'failing to thrive'. Despite a few anxious moments in Indonesia we arrived home safely. Lactose intolerance was the culprit and Rini soon began to blossom.

Just over two years later and we were back in Indonesia. This time we had set out to adopt an older child, preferably a boy. After considerable delays and several false starts we connected with our new son, Daniel. Or rather, *he* met *us* in the airport terminal in Surabaya and instantly set about carrying our bags! Daniel was, by all accounts, 13 years old. We later reduced his age by two years, something we have never regretted, although he did have to wait an extra two years to become an adult.

Thus, by mid 1982, we were a family of five. We had been on the roller-coaster ride for seven years and little did we realise it was only the beginning.

My greatest worry when considering adoption initially concerned the possibility of absolute integration and acceptance of Asian-born children into our white Anglo-Saxon family. Both the children's grandfathers were World War II veterans who had experienced combat first hand against the Japanese in the Pacific. They put their prejudices aside and our children became integrally their grandchildren with no reservations and all the hoped-for mutual rewards. I considered every other worry to be surmountable and secondary.

The challenges were many. Initially just adapting to parenthood; then the trauma of a burns accident and the resultant guilt; a tiny baby with severe lactose intolerance; integrating a teenager into the family at a time when normal teenage development dictates 'detachment' rather than 'attachment'; the difficulties associated with educating a child whose prior education was limited and so very different; transiting through a separation and divorce trying to ensure the least possible impact on the children; 'normal' adolescence; adapting to a lifelong illness and the usual normal cycle of life and death as it affected our family. We have weathered them all and each of the children has steadily matured and developed, in understanding of self and others.

My greatest joy comes from knowing that through adoption our children have choices that they almost certainly would not have otherwise had. They have access to medical treatment, good food, a warm bed and someone always there who will listen and love them when the going gets rough. And I have shared in their joyous moments, been introduced to their friends as 'my mum', and laughed and cried with them.

I have remained integrally involved with intercountry adoption for the 30 years of my adoption journey. Adoption has been a positive through all our lives. As children they loved to retrace their story through photos and story telling, each year making appropriate additions as they grew in understanding.

I have two equally important pieces of advice for prospective adoptive parents. Firstly, don't be afraid to *parent* your children. We are the adults and must make responsible (not necessarily popular) decisions for our children until they are genuinely ready to assume the adult role. Being a responsible parent is far more important than trying to keep a child 'happy' all the time. Secondly, keep in regular touch with other adoptive families and children, let your children experience being the 'same' as others, rather than 'different'; let them see they are not 'the only onion in the petunia patch' but rather, 'a beautiful petunia in a beautiful petunia patch'!

My three petunias are not perfect—because they are human. But each one is, I believe, a nice person, an asset to society and importantly, a credit to themselves. I have been lucky enough to be part of each one's journey which, in turn, has made me a better person.

My 'children' are currently 34, 28 and 25. It is Easter Sunday and we sit around the table talking. It is nice to have all three home at the one time as it doesn't happen much these days. They have all read this story and have started making comments regarding their own challenges, their highs and lows.

All are positive about being adopted, basically for the same general reason: the choices made available due to increased educational opportunities, family support and encouragement. Daniel added that as an older adopted child he really appreciates the feeling of belonging and the freedom that adoption has given him. Daniel is a uniformed soldier in the Salvation Army, which is interesting as he was raised in Salvation Army orphanages from the age of two days until we adopted him. Now nearly 34 he states that he has that sense of belonging – with his adoptive family and with his church community. He considers freedom of thought, speech and worship important and also commented that he is not restricted by extreme poverty, as he may otherwise have been.

Racism has not been a big issue with any of them, but all three have experienced some. At primary school Rini was frequently called 'Abo'. Tuti made the comment that when people say things about Asians she feels included, though friends often add that she is 'different from them' (Asians). Both girls find these mixed messages difficult to come to terms with.

Daniel continues to speak fluent Indonesian but Tuti (and Rini to a lesser extent) feel some embarrassment that they cannot speak their birth language. When people know they were born in Indonesia they expect them to speak the language. Tuti went on to say that she gets a bit tired of explaining and spelling her name.

Daniel has met his biological parents and some half-siblings in latter years. His experience in his own words was 'not good' and he has real reservations about encouraging others to seek out their biological roots. Perhaps it is partly a consequence of this experience that leads both the girls to say that they have no interest at all in searching, though both agreed it would be interesting to see relatives from a distance, to see what they looked like and whether there is a resemblance. Both the girls also commented that their interest is more with siblings than with parents.

Accepting and facing the consequences of living with a long-term illness (that could be seen by some as a disability) was and still is an enormous challenge for Rini. Paradoxically it is that situation that has led to strong family bonds and a sense of thankfulness for adoption. In her previous circumstances it is doubtful that the medical assistance that allows her to lead a normal, fulfilling life would have been available.

All three agreed that the separation and subsequent divorce of their adoptive parents almost 20 years ago was a huge trauma at the time, as has been the experience of the deaths of close relatives and friends since then. All have been significant stressors for them, impacting on what could be seen as already fragile souls, having all experienced major losses earlier in their lives.

To see them together is an absolute joy and to hear them talk so openly and personally about adoption and its impact is a credit to each of them. It seems to me that we are all the lucky ones in this adoption story.

This is part of a poem I wrote during our journey.

> Abstract dream, truly reality
> Beautiful child
> Our child.
>
> Mother
> I mourn your loss
> But I can never know
> Your true feelings
>
> Mother
> Trust me.

Contributors

Wendy M. Anderson lives in Melbourne. She describes herself as a slow learner, marrying just a week before her thirtieth birthday and becoming a new parent the week of her fortieth. She began her adult life as a teacher, reinvented herself in a publishing house, and then moved on to her current incarnation as a mother and freelancer. She says the best things in her life came pre-loved – her husband and step-son, and two Korean-born children. Her children say she talks too much. Her husband says she doesn't write enough. She says thank you for giving life to her story by being its audience.

Elisha Barrow lives in Reynella, south of Adelaide. She worked as a veterinary nurse with her husband, a vet, until 2001 when they adopted their first child, a girl, from Korea. Elisha has since been busy at home with their daughter, and their son who arrived from Thailand in 2005. She and her husband are hoping for a further update to this biography by 2007, as their file to adopt their third child is ready to go to China. Elisha enjoys family life and is very involved in her children's pre-school and school. She also enjoys children's literature and hopes to pursue this interest as her children grow up.

Peta Brindusa lives in Western Australia and was the first single woman in Western Australia to adopt. While the process was gruelling, time consuming and emotional she found it all worth-while once she was allocated her beautiful little boy from Romania. Peta now lives with her son, his new puppy and his ferret, Stretchy. Yes, a ferret! Both Peta and James would love to adopt again but unfortunately finances cannot stretch that far. They are grateful to have each other and enjoy every moment that life has to offer.

Emma Caldwell lives in rural Victoria with her husband, two children and a number of pets. She works from home as a casual book-keeper when she has time and enjoys reading, jigsaws, crosswords, the computer/Internet and spending time with her family.

Charmaine Cooper lives in Port Lincoln with her husband, children and much-loved dog. They are an active family and love the beach, sport and – of course – travelling. Ethiopia is very much a part of their lives. Charmaine raises money to support the Addis Ababa Fistula Hospital, in between running after kids, sport and helping in the classroom and with the family business.

Maxine Donald lives in the Barossa Valley in South Australia with her husband and 90-year-old mother. Her three adult children live in Adelaide. In 1977, Maxine was among the first South Australians to adopt through the Indonesian court system. She and her (first) husband were among the first childless couples to adopt from overseas, as prior to this many overseas adoptions occurred for humanitarian reasons within families with children. Maxine has a background in education but has been working in overseas adoption and post-adoption support since the 1970s. Through her experiences she has a keen understanding of the needs of adoptive parents and a strong empathy with older adoptees. Apart from her family and her work Maxine enjoys painting and photography.

Jo-Anne Duffield lives with her husband, Stephen, and three daughters in Crystal Brook, 200 kilometres north of Adelaide. She and her husband run their own business and Jo-Anne is very involved in the children's lives: kindergarten, school, dancing, netball, Guides, basketball and swimming. She also finds time to be involved as co-ordinator of the Indian Family and Friends network which offers support and friendship to other families going through the adoption process with India.

Louise Gale lives in suburbia with her family. Life is busy with three children and the many activities that revolve around them, as well as part-time work. Other than writing Louise enjoys reading, web surfing, gardening, dreaming about travelling, sharing and learning more about adoption, scrap booking, and having long cups of tea with friends.

Joanne Howitt-Smith trained as a nursing sister in the late 1970s. She married, had two children and together with her first husband built up a medium-sized retail company. Jo commenced her Bachelor of Arts in Psychology at the age of 30 and remarried in 1997, acquiring two stepchildren. Twin girls from Ethiopia joined their family in 2002. She and her husband now have six children and four grandchildren! Apart from her family and her faith, Jo's passions include writing, quilting and preserving her family's history and photographs. Jo has also worked as a family support worker for the adoption agency in South Australia in the post-placement team.

Anthea Hunt is a mother of two sons and three daughters. Their turn-of-the-century home is in a seaside suburb of Adelaide. Anthea works part-time as a registered nurse in aged care and as an aromatherapist. She has a long-standing and active passion for social justice, environmental issues and Australian fauna. She enjoys drawing and painting for pleasure and relaxation.

Marilyn Jacobs was born in Adelaide in 1950 and studied music and education. She has worked as a teacher and in the educational counselling and rehabilitation fields. Since adopting her daughter from Thailand she has resigned from full-time employment to devote more time to her family and creative pursuits.

Deb Levett-Olson works as a counsellor and teacher in a state junior primary school where young new arrivals, including adoptees, migrants and refugees, are introduced to school. Her partner, a church minister, is also involved in education. Apart from her daily fitness walks with two lively and demanding dogs and bushwalking when time allows, Deb has a strong interest in global politics and justice issues. She enjoys films, reading, travel, and red wine (not necessarily in that order).

Claire Laishley is married to Garry and has three children. She lives in Glenelg East in South Australia. Claire's book *My mother is my daughter*, published in 2002, tells the story of her emotional journey when her mother was diagnosed with Alzheimer's. Claire is working on her second non-fiction book after receiving encouragement from a South Australian publishing company. She also writes short stories and articles, and is secretary of the Seaside Writers' Group.

Virginia Ruth Leigh lives with her husband in the north-eastern suburbs of Adelaide, with their two adult children, adopted in the late sixties, and grandchildren living nearby. They are enjoying an 'astonishingly active' semi-retirement. Virginia has always been interested in writing, and for five years edited the national newsletter for a community support group for women with Turner syndrome. She is currently studying Professional Writing.

Lyne Moore lives in Perth, Western Australia, with her husband Rick and her two sons, Dean and Carl. Lyne works part-time and cherishes every moment spent with her husband and sons.

Susan Lomman is a mother of one, and formerly of Adelaide, South Australia. Susan adopted Ashleigh in October 2002. Susan has worked as a radiographer in a private practice but is currently studying junior primary/primary teaching.

Melina Magdalena lives in Adelaide with her two children. She migrated to Australia at the age of four, and comes from a cultur-ally diverse family. She identifies as Jewish Australian. She has a degree in linguistics and German, a certificate in sign writing, and is currently studying education. Melina supports her family through whatever work she can pick up, and spends her time writing and creating, as well as putting a great deal of voluntary energy into various women's and human rights community projects.

Deborah 'Deb' McDowall is a sleep-deprived, stay-at-home mother of two beautiful boys who enjoys moulding play dough farm animals, dancing to Hi-5 and the Wiggles, building double-decker sandcastles, reading *Dr Seuss* out loud, and scraping petrified food off the dining-room windows and floor. In days gone by, when she was true to her astrological sign (Capricorn), she managed the staff development service at a private hospital with great attention to detail, relentless busyness, undying determination, and abundant energy. These days she directs the flow less, and goes with the flow more. Despite endless debate over whose turn it is to sleep-in on the weekends and tantrum management strategies, she remains a devoted and loving wife to her husband, John. Every day she is thankful for the joy her two children bring to her life, and to all those who brought them to her, and hopeful for a peaceful night's sleep. The family currently reside in Queensland.

Susan 'Sue' Olsen grew up in the lower Blue Mountains and returned to the upper Blue Mountains after adopting her two children. There she and her husband Ian built their own home. Her life now encompasses writing, yoga, meditation, bushwalking, family, and a love of tall ships. She describes herself as 'semi retired' and 'temporarily grounded'. She and Ian run bush cabins, and they look forward to many more adventures and travels in the years to come.

Andrew Rate lives in Perth with his wife. In December 2004, after this story was written, they were waiting to travel to Anhui Province, China, to meet their adopted daughter. Andrew has been writing poetry since childhood, but had never ventured into writing prose before submitting material for this anthology. He has published poetry in *Studio: a journal of christians writing* and *Yellow Moon*, and in 2000 won the Catalpa Writers' Prize for poetry. He also enjoys playing guitar and communing with nature, and his weekday life is occupied as a lecturer in earth science at the University of Western Australia. Unfortunately, he is not '30-something' any more.

Julia Rollings lives in Canberra with her husband, Barry, and their eight children: Alix, Briony, Madhu, Haden, Joel, Sadan, Akil and Sabila, and numerous pets. When not at home dealing with copious amounts of laundry and cooking, she works as a case-worker in a therapeutic residential program for adolescents with complex and challenging behaviour.

Madhu Rollings came to Australia in April 1995 from central India. He completed Year 12 in 2004 and is currently working as a second year apprentice air-conditioning and refrigeration technician.

Lisa Saxby lives near the Barossa Valley in South Australia with her husband, son, and new daughter from China. The family has a wide circle of friends, many of whom they have met through adoption. They enjoy participating in activities that celebrate their children's birth cultures, both Korean and Chinese. A very happy family of four, they haven't yet ruled out the possibility of adding to their family again through intercountry adoption.

Pam Sharpe emigrated from the UK to Perth in 1999. She is Professor of History at the University of Tasmania in Hobart and researches the history of women, gender and families among other subjects in the social and economic history of England. She has published and edited a number of academic books and articles in scholarly journals.

Belinda Shaw grew up in Adelaide and married Tim in 1991. They moved to Darwin in 1997 and love living in the Top End. In 1999 Rachel arrived from India and in 2003, Jacob from Korea. This is the first time Belinda has written for a book and she has enjoyed it very much. She is a working mum and spending time with her family is very important. Belinda also loves quilting, entertaining, and relaxing.

Bessie Smith lives in South Australia with her husband, son and three cats. Her step-daughter spends school holidays with them. Bessie works part-time as a nurse. Best times are watching her son play sports and rollerblading, going to the movies together and spending time away on family holidays.

Katie Stewart lives in Irishtown, near Northam, in Western Australia. She and her husband and three children, aged 13, seven and three, run a wheat/sheep farm and have an assortment of pets including two dogs, two cats and two ducks. Before becoming a mum, Katie was a teacher. Now she is an artist (mainly landscapes, commissioned pet portraits and book illustrations) and a would-be writer. She is currently the editor of the local adoption support group newsletter.

Fiona Thorogood is married to Darren and they live in a rural area just outside of Mt Gambier in the South East of Australia. Fiona currently works part-time at the local general store but has a nursing background. Fiona and her family are involved in post-adoption support, being coordinators of their local adoption support group as well as the Indian Family and Friends Group, a state-wide support group that meets twice a year in Adelaide. Darren is a project officer at an electricity distribution company. Once both of the girls are in school Fiona will consider returning to nursing after a refresher course. For now she is enjoying being a full-time mum.

Janine 'Neen' Weir lives in Paddington, New South Wales, with her husband Adam, their three Korean-Australian children, and their pet hungarian vizsla, Felix. Neen and Adam's journey toward their 'forever family' began as a discussion in 1997 after watching a state government information video. Jett Joon Ha joined the family in 2001, Joon Woo in 2003 (both intercountry adoption) and Yoo Jung in 2005 (local adoption after relinquishment by previous adoptive family). All children comprehend English and Korean equally, with two of them attending a Korean preschool. Neen continues to study Korean. The family travels regularly to South Korea.

Acknowledgements

I would like to thank the contributors to this anthology for their preparedness to share their stories for the benefit of others. And to their children, I hope these stories provide rich insights.

Many thanks to the readers of early drafts: Carmel Hemmings, Sue Priest, Maxine Donald.

Thanks to Alan Hoare for the photography.

And thanks to Julia Beaven for her sharp editing and to the team at Wakefield Press, especially Clinton for typesetting and layout, and Liz for the cover design.

Poinciana

Jane Turner Goldsmith

'Café au lait' *she calls him, the young nurse who finds him in the wet mud on the riverbank, hours after his birth. He is too shocked to wail, would have died in the tunnel of bamboo leaves feathering gently above him.*

Catherine Piron is in Nouméa, searching for traces of the father she barely remembers. She meets journalist Henri Boulez, her only lead in a foreign country. Their journey into the remote regions of New Caledonia uncovers an extraordinary story that, like the island itself, *brille à la fois claire et noire au soleil* – shimmers light and dark in the sun.

ISBN 978 1 86254 699 8

For more information visit www.wakefieldpress.com.au

The Rollercoaster

A country couple's ride with in-vitro fertilisation

Julia Masters

At the clinic a familiar nurse greeted us and showed us into an unfamiliar room. It had a huge framed Monet print, a stack of magazines and a bed with stirrups.

The in-vitro fertilisation program introduces farmers Julia and Lester Masters to a mixture of delightful possibilities and medical evil necessities. Content in their marriage and their work, they begin treatment optimistically. Their desire to bear a child becomes even stronger once they have conceived children, albeit in a laboratory. But as they pursue this desire the logistics of running a farm and undergoing treatment become ever more difficult, and they find that infertility affects their lives and their attitudes in ways they could not have imagined.

The Rollercoaster, a very personal and moving book, shows what involvement in IVF is really like. Honest and engaging, it takes the reader from days working with the Masters on their farm to the couple's first view of a tiny human embryo. Julia Masters' story will surprise anyone accustomed to media portrayals of IVF.

ISBN 978 1 86254 485 7

For more information visit www.wakefieldpress.com.au

Siblings

Brothers and sisters of children with special needs

Kate Strohm

Siblings tells what it is like to grow up with a sister or brother who has a disability or chronic illness. The siblings of children with special needs are often the overlooked ones in families struggling to cope.

Kate Strohm, an experienced health professional and journalist who has a sister with cerebral palsy, bravely shares the story of her journey from confusion and distress to greater understanding and acceptance. She also provides a forum for other siblings to describe their struggles with resentment, guilt, grief and isolation, their fears and also their joys.

Besides giving siblings a voice at last, Kate Strohm also provides strategies that siblings themselves, parents and practitioners can use to support brothers and sisters of children with special needs.

ISBN 978 1 86254 580 9

For more information visit www.wakefieldpress.com.au

Someone You Know

A friend's farewell

Maria Pallotta-Chiarolli

Someone You Know is Maria Pallotta-Chiarolli's biography of Jon, who is living with AIDS, and the story of their extraordinary friendship. Maria and Jon teach together, hold common views; they also share secrets. The threads and entanglements of their lives come together at Jon's final gathering.

'I have rarely been so moved by a piece of writing, in a book or on stage or screen, as I was by the end of *Someone You Know*.' *Age*

'It's the story of a friendship, of insights into gay life, of a journey that ends in death, but also in birth, in spiritual growth and understanding. It's true, and it's the story of someone you know.'
AIDS Council of South Australia

ISBN 978 1 86254 271 6

For more information visit www.wakefieldpress.com.au

Lifelines

Breaking out of Locked-in Syndrome

Jane Turner Goldsmith

While on a business trip to Singapore in 1992, 41-year-old Peter Couche, an Australian stockbroker based in London and father of three, suffered an irreversible brain-stem stroke. Twenty-four hours later he was paralysed: he could blink in response to questions but was unable to speak, eat or breathe independently, although his mind remained alert.

It took more than thirteen years for Peter to record this inspiring story of his struggle for a normal life, away from the mind-numbing world of institutions.

Lifelines is a love story and an account of the hope provided by stem-cell therapy. Above all Peter Couche shows how miracles can happen if we fight hard enough.

Of all the qualities with which I have had to arm myself, patience, persistence and a positive attitude have been the most important — they are such precious qualities. And so is laughter, the life-giving power of laughter. These are my lifelines. Peter Couche

ISBN 978 1 86254 767 4

For more information visit www.wakefieldpress.com.au

Wakefield Press is an independent publishing and
distribution company based in Adelaide, South Australia.
We love good stories and publish beautiful books.
To see our full range of titles, please visit our website at
www.wakefieldpress.com.au.